D1595690

COLUMBIA/HCA—
HEALTHCARE
ON OVERDRIVE

COLUMBIA/HCA— HEALTHCARE ON OVERDRIVE

SANDY LUTZ

E. PRESTON GEE

HFMA® Healthcare Financial Management Association

Educational Foundation

McGraw-Hill

New York   San Francisco   Washington, D.C.   Auckland   Bogotá
Caracas   Lisbon   London   Madrid   Mexico City   Milan
Montreal   New Delhi   San Juan   Singapore
Sydney   Tokyo   Toronto

McGraw-Hill

*A Division of The **McGraw·Hill** Companies*

Copyright © 1998 by McGraw-Hill. All rights reserved. Printed in the United States of America. Except as permitted under the United States Copyright Act of 1976, no part of this publication may be reproduced or distributed in any form or by any means, or stored in a database or retrieval system, without the prior written permission of the publisher.

1 2 3 4 5 6 7 8 9 0 BKM / BKM 02 01 00 99 98

ISBN 0-07024804-4

Printed and bound by Book-mart Press, Inc.

This publication is designed to provide accurate and authoritative information in regard to the subject matter covered. It is sold with the understanding that neither the author nor the publisher is engaged in rendering legal, accounting, or other professional service. If legal advice or other expert assistance is required, the services of a competent professional person should be sought.
> *—From a Declaration of Principles jointly adapted by a Committee of the American Bar Association and a Committee of Publishers.*

McGraw-Hill books are available at special quantity discounts to use as premiums and sales promotions, or for use in corporate training programs. For more information, please write to the Director of Sales, McGraw-Hill, 11 West 19th Street, New York, NY 10011. Or contact your local bookstore.

Library of Congress Cataloging-in-Publication Data

Lutz, Sandy
   Columbia/HCA—healthcare on overdrive /
Sandy Lutz, E. Preston Gee.
     p.   cm.
   Rev. and expanded ed. of: The for-profit healthcare revolution, © 1995.
   Includes index.
   ISBN 0–07024804–4
   1. Columbia/HCA Healthcare Corporation. 2. Medical corporations—
United States. I. Gee, Erin Preston. II. Lutz, Sandy. For-profit healthcare
revolution. III. Title.
R728.2.L874   1997
362′.1′0425—dc21   97-44835
                                                CIP

CONTENTS

INTRODUCTION

This book represents an expanded revision of *The For-Profit Healthcare Revolution,* written in 1995 and published by Irwin Professional Publishing (now owned by McGraw-Hill). The original book was published during the fall of 1995.

We decided the book needed a major overhaul in early 1997. However, we never anticipated the events of the summer of 1997, especially the federal investigation that enveloped Columbia/HCA and led to the ouster of its two leading executives, Rick Scott and David Vandewater. That series of events, which began in March with the FBI "raid" on Columbia facilities in El Paso, received nearly as much media coverage and national publicity as the healthcare reform movement of 1994. However, the Columbia coverage was more dramatic and therefore arguably more engaging than most political maneuvering in Washington.

Consequently, this revision owes much of its added bulk and updated observations to the events surrounding the "search and seige," as one pundit called it, involving Columbia/HCA. Therein lies the relevance, as well as possible insight into the future direction of the entire segment of the healthcare industry known as the for-profit sector. Admittedly, this book is about all the major players in the for-profit sector, along with their history, philosophy, and in some cases, scrutiny. However, because of the heavy publicity surrounding the federal investigation, much of the public is aware that Columbia/HCA is an amalgam of several previous systems; apropos of its grandiose name, it is a large organizational body made up of several tributaries, including Hospital Corporation of America (HCA), Galen Health Care, HealthTrust, and Epic. In a similar fashion, the second largest for-profit chain, Tenet Healthcare Corporation, is a combination of two large systems, National Medical Enterprises (NME) and American Medical International (AMI). Consequently, the history of all the large chains is essential background for understanding the operating style and corporate philosophy of the contemporary titans of healthcare.

Most of the additional material included in this edition involves Columbia's triumphs and trials from 1995 to 1997. There has rarely been a political force or market factor that has galvanized the public's interest in healthcare like the events surrounding Columbia/HCA, which serves as the focal point of this book.

Bold and brash, Columbia executives always handled things in a unique style, including the events that led to their undoing. Although the Columbia momentum appears to be slowing down, there are lessons for the entire nation, particularly the participants in America's healthcare system. In truth, the story of Columbia is not so much about a colossally ambitious company, nor its now-fabled aggressive chieftains. It is the broader story of America's failure to come to grips with the true nature and optimal structure of this country's largest service industry—healthcare. The reform movement of the early 1990s awakened a powerful force within healthcare—the for-profit visionaries who believed the answer to reforming the system was market-driven, not politically mandated. However, through all the market-driven reform of the mid-1990s, there remained strong and irreversible undercurrents of societal and political sentiment regarding the nation's healthcare system. Given some of these fundamental attitudes as a backdrop, the story of for-profit founders and their firms is all the more engaging and potentially illuminating into what the future holds for the United States' healthcare system.

Although this book was not written solely about Columbia/HCA, much of the text, especially the added chapters, focuses on the Nashville behemoth. However, because Columbia is an amalgam of several of the original for-profit firms, the history and chronology of all the investor-owned systems are highly relevant.

The first chapter of this book deals with the history and philosophy of the founding fathers of the for-profit movement and the firms they incorporated. Since the relatively brief tenure of investor-owned chains has seen several permutations and reconfigurations of these firms (and may yet see more such combinations), the past is relevant as a predictor of the future.

Chapter 2 outlines the genesis and early years of Columbia, and details the events leading to its role as consolidator and amalgamator of its predecessors. Chapter 3 picks up where *The For-Profit Healthcare Revolution* left off, with the ambitious strategy and aggressive style that have characterized Columbia's image in recent months. Chapter 4 begins to chronicle Columbia's challenges with the government investigation, media scrutiny, and other associated problems, leading to the eventual resignation of Rick Scott and David Vandewater. Chapter 5 highlights the early days and weeks of Dr. Thomas Frist Jr. as the new Chairman and Chief Executive Officer (CEO) of Columbia/HCA and contrasts the approach and philosophy of the new executive team.

Chapter 6 discusses the other for-profit systems, including Tenet, which promises to be a significant player in the future given Columbia/HCA's present strategy to slow down its growth. Chapter 7 takes a reflective look at the lessons learned from the Columbia/HCA experience. The concluding section of the book, Chapter 8, attempts to look into the future and assess the implications for the industry, its investors, and the American public, as well as the primary subject of the book, Columbia/HCA Healthcare Corporation.

ACKNOWLEDGMENTS

We would like to acknowledge the contribution of the many individuals at Columbia/HCA Healthcare Corporation, as well as many others who have worked at for-profit hospital chains.

We express our sincere gratitude to the many individuals whom we interviewed for this book, and who offered valuable insight and perspective on the history and future of the for-profit sector. There are too many to list, but they are cited throughout the text.

Finally, we are indebted to our spouses, Janice Gee and Larry Lutz, for their patience and endurance while the book was being completed.

PROLOGUE

Ousting a CEO is never easy. It's even more difficult when he's taken an investment of $250,000 and built a company worth over $20 billion in less than a decade. This is quite an accomplishment for anyone, but especially for the CEO in question: a 44-year-old son of a truck driver from Kansas City, who used to sit in the back of the classroom (so he wouldn't be noticed), yet was listed as one of *TIME* magazine's 25 most influential people in 1995.

But on the night of July 24, 1997, the board of Columbia/HCA Healthcare Corporation had to set aside the remarkable achievements of its Chairman and CEO, Richard Scott, and focus on the matters at hand. The company that Scott built (or at least assembled) was under investigation by the government, under siege by the media, and under pressure from the shareholders.

From the board's standpoint, the solution to the present dilemma was painful but obvious—Scott and his right-hand man (Columbia's President and Chief Operating Officer [COO], David Vandewater), had to go. So the board advanced that proposal to the hard-driving Missourian. Scott resisted at first, but he eventually succumbed to the inevitable. Although a lawyer by trade, in what was undoubtedly the most important argument he would present, he was unable to persuade the "jury" of his peers.

The resignations of Scott and Vandewater closed one of the most fascinating chapters in the history of American business. The story of Rick Scott and Columbia/HCA is an engaging tale that combines the real-life dimensions of a modern-day Horatio Alger with the hardball realities of taking on the venerable world of American healthcare. What's more, the Columbia/HCA experience highlights a defining chapter in the ongoing story of America's largest service industry and the role and relevance of for-profit healthcare systems within that industry.

1

CHAPTER

The For-Profit Founders and Their Firms

You couldn't lose money.

Joel Gordon, founder, General Care Corporation, commenting on the early days of for-profit healthcare

The story of Columbia/HCA Healthcare Corporation is not the story of one company or of one man. Instead, it is the story of many hospital companies that converged into the single largest provider of healthcare in the United States. Columbia grew through merger after merger. Its mass came primarily through the work of for-profit executives who had tilled the ground long before Richard Scott saw the potential of this enterprise.

Shakespeare told us the past is prologue. Today's corporate hospital titans are testament to that, building their empires on foundations created by investor-owned hospital firms in the 1960s. Today, some 1,300 hospitals are investor-owned hospitals, meaning that they are owned by companies or individuals who answer to shareholders or other investors. These companies, which own about 20 percent of the nation's hospitals and 15 percent of the nation's 1.2 million hospital beds, also pay taxes.

3

The rest of the nation's hospitals are not-for-profit. They are the Baptist, Methodist, Catholic, and County Memorial hospitals of America. Some were founded more than 125 years ago by communities, church groups, or government entities.

Hospitals are the hub of today's trillion-dollar healthcare industry. Outpatient services, home healthcare, and physician services spin off and around that hub, but hospitals take home the lion's share—40 cents of every healthcare dollar. Oddly enough, other segments of the healthcare industry aren't dominated by not-for-profit organizations. Most nursing homes, home healthcare agencies, pharmaceutical companies, and physician groups are taxpaying, for-profit organizations, in contrast with hospitals.

While the differences between "for-profit" and "not-for-profit" hospitals used to be clear-cut, they are becoming less so. Critics of investor-owned systems charge that they care more about profits than quality patient care. Critics of not-for-profit systems say those hospitals don't provide enough charity care and community service to deserve their tax exemptions.

Arguably, in recent years, not-for-profit hospitals have started acting more like for-profit ones, adopting some of their business-school efficiencies and management techniques. Meanwhile, investor-owned hospitals have taken on some of the qualities of not-for-profit institutions, providing charity care and community service. In some cases, they have no choice. By federal law, no hospital, whether owned by the community or stockholders, can turn away emergency patients regardless of their ability to pay. This sometimes extends to nonemergency patients. In some small towns, the only hospital is investor-owned, making it hard to refuse medical care to a patient who can't pay.

In the near future, "it will be difficult to tell the not-for-profits and the investor-owned hospitals apart," predicts Robert O'Leary, former president of one of the nation's largest investor-owned chains (American Medical International) and prior to that, of the largest not-for-profit hospital alliance (Voluntary Hospitals of America). O'Leary now heads Premier, a San Diego–based alliance with over 1,000 not-for-profit hospitals.

He believes not-for-profit hospital systems will begin accessing the equity market. The alliance he now manages has a venture capital arm that invests in emerging technologies. Investor-owned chains, O'Leary believes, will see value in responding to a community's entire health needs. He maintains that they will focus on "providing care and treat profits as a derivative."

GOVERNMENT-PROMPTED REFORM

President Clinton tried to revolutionize the healthcare system in 1994, but his plan didn't get far in Congress. Nonetheless, the revolution did occur. His blueprint that fostered purchasing alliances inspired hundreds of hospitals to look for partners. If hospitals were to be forced to negotiate with large purchasing alliances, they needed to combine their clout. The desire to merge or be acquired reached a high point in 1994 when over 650 hospitals (more than 10 percent of all U.S. hospitals) were caught up in merger and acquisition deals.

The Clinton plan wasn't the only impetus, though. If the Clinton plan was the spark, for-profit companies were the gasoline. Even when deals didn't involve them, the threat of the Columbia/HCA Healthcare Corporation or another investor-owned chain coming into their markets galvanized hospital boards into action. What was the result? Like shares of IBM or futures in cotton, hospitals became a commodity controlled by larger and larger corporations. Hospital corporations were born in the 1960s and went through a retrenchment and restructuring period in the mid-1980s after Medicare introduced a new prospective payment system. Then, during the early 1990s, they entered a period of resurgence.

In each case, the nation's economy and government policy played roles in how these companies fared. Some would argue that what's happening now is just another reconfiguration. The question on the minds of investors and industry experts is, "Will the pieces that stacked together to build Columbia into the nation's largest healthcare provider collapse into a heap of different shapes in the foreseeable future?" This is an industry that has basically recycled itself within a span of 30 years. Yet, in spite of the industry's rise and fall and rise again, a small circle of survivors seems to hang in there.

"There have been four different periods since 1968 that people said, 'Boy, you'd better get out of the hospital business. You're in trouble,'" said Thomas Frist Jr., M.D., who founded Hospital Corporation of America (HCA) and recently took over Columbia/HCA following Rick Scott's resignation. Despite the warnings, the Nashville surgeon-turned-businessman didn't get out. In fact, he found that adversity created opportunity. That was true in 1994—one of the industry's most uncertain years because of Clinton's much ballyhooed promise to reform the nation's healthcare system. Yet, while healthcare reform crashed and burned in the nation's capital, investor-owned chains were aggressively buying hospitals. Even not-for-profit systems were eyeing competitors to buy.

More than any other year in the past decade, 1994 altered the fabric of the healthcare business in America's cities and towns. During that year, investor-owned chains, most notably Columbia, developed a disturbing predilection to "covet thy neighbor's hospital." This didn't necessarily sit well with many in the not-for-profit dominated industry that cherished the collegial relationships of the past.

Take for instance this lead from a news article in the *Orlando Sentinel* on March 25, 1995: "A document released Friday by a federal magistrate in Orlando appears to show a national hospital chain [Columbia] plotting to upset the balance of power among the region's largest hospitals." Plotting to upset the balance of power among the region's largest hospitals? Such headlines and speculation gave cause to wonder what calculated power move Columbia would make next.

In another extract, from the *San Diego Union*, March 16, 1995: "The nation's largest for-profit hospital chain [again, Columbia] has set its sights on buying control of hospitals and physician groups here, which could radically alter a regional marketplace dominated by non-profit, community hospitals." As the adage goes, the meek may inherit the earth, but they'll never gain much market share. Investor-owned companies such as Columbia have long been bad-mouthed and often ignored by the not-for-profit hospital sector. Purportedly, they skim the cream by treating only affluent patients, turn away the indigent, and drive up costs, or so the critics say.

In the past 20 years, some things have not changed. For-profit hospitals still get their share of bad-mouthing. However, they are no longer ignored. When a few men started for-profit hospital companies in the late 1960s, the thought of turning a profit on healthcare was considered anathema by those on the "respectable" not-for-profit-side. After all, the traditionalists argued, people's lives are at stake in these institutions; profits shouldn't be a motivation.

In fact, some local hospital associations blackballed for-profit hospitals as recently as the 1980s. A turning point came, however, when David Jones yanked the $333,000 membership of his Humana hospitals from the American Hospital Association (AHA) in December 1985. Humana, a Louisville, Kentucky-grown hospital chain, was a mighty power at the time. Jones, Humana's founder (and a former Golden Gloves boxer), believed his company wasn't getting its money's worth from the AHA. Why fake a punch when you can jab? For not-for-profit executives, Jones's move was a wake-up call. Not only could for-profit chains threaten to use their economic clout to weaken national associations, but they would also follow through on their threats.

In the end, the not-for-profit hospitals that dominated the AHA succumbed to giving membership discounts to investor-owned chains of hospitals. Humana rejoined. Today, for-profit executives filter through state and national hospital groups, participating fully. It's hard to imagine these leaders not being included.

THOSE WHO FAIL TO LEARN THE LESSONS OF HISTORY . . .

In the hospital industry, it often seems as though only the moment exists. Individuals and hospitals get pushed down like a

cork in the water, then later bob to the surface again, in a different place, with different circumstances. As the saying goes,
you can't keep a good man (or even a scoundrel, for that matter)
down.

Since the industry's growth isn't well chronicled, is it
doomed to repeat the mistakes of the past? When asked what
today's generation of hospital companies learned from the previous generation, a CEO of a top hospital chain answered,
"Zero." He went on to say that, "In the past, the span of control
of hospitals has been about 100 hospitals. When they run over
100, they get into trouble." That may have been a prophetic comment given the troubles Columbia encountered starting in the
spring of 1997.

Such an observation is especially chilling considering that
Columbia/HCA accounted for nearly one-third of the investor-
owned industry following its $5.6 billion acquisition of
HealthTrust in 1995. In other words, Columbia practically dominated a movement that has been viewed as a battering ram in
one of the nation's largest industries.

Throughout the merger mania of the mid-1990s, industry
observers debated the question, "Could Columbia (now the nation's seventh largest employer) become a General Motors for
the healthcare industry?" Just as three automotive companies
dominate the U.S. automotive industry, could Columbia, Tenet,
and a few other healthcare companies direct the future of this
trillion-dollar sector? If the past is indeed prologue, Columbia
was destined to grow to a massive size. Then it would break up
in a wave of divestitures and restructuring—that is, if the brief
history of privately owned healthcare companies were to repeat
itself. Columbia executives say that probably won't happen;
their company (which during 1994, according to *Fortune*
magazine, was the nation's fourteenth fastest growing corporation) is different. Yet, looking at investor-owned chains of the
past, it's wise to never say never, or perhaps, never say forever.

Perhaps the best illustration of this industry dynamic can
be observed by considering the list of publicly held hospital
companies in 1984. The ensuing financial and organizational

chaos makes several years seem like a lifetime in the world of investor-owned chains.

- American Medical International—acquired in 1995 by National Medical Enterprises, which later changed its name to Tenet Healthcare Corporation.
- Basic American Medical—purchased by Columbia Hospital Corporation (which later became Columbia/HCA) in 1992.
- Charter Medical Corporation—went through bankruptcy reorganization after a leveraged buyout, as the overbuilt psychiatric market financially crippled the company. Became Magellan Health Corporation following a merger with a managed mental healthcare company. Magellan subsequently sold the real estate for the psychiatric hospitals to a real estate investment trust and spun off the operations to a separate company.
- Community Psychiatric Centers—battered by the slump in the industry; transformed itself into a Transitional Hospitals Corporation, which operated long-term care hospitals, an industry sector that pays better than psychiatric care. Transitional later sold to Vencor, a long-term care company in Louisville, Kentucky.
- Comprehensive Care Corporation—nearly exited the hospital business; another casualty of payors' perception that psychiatric hospitals were running up their charges in the late 1980s.
- HEI Corporation—bought by Columbia in 1990.
- Hospital Corporation of America—merged with Columbia in 1994.
- Humana—broke into two parts in 1993, an insurance company and a hospital company. Columbia bought its hospitals, under the new name of Galen Health Care, in 1993.
- National Medical Enterprises—hit bottom in 1994 with restructuring, lawsuits, federal criminal investigations,

and financial problems, but emerged as one of the major players. Acquired AMI in 1995 and changed its name to Tenet Healthcare Corporation.

- Nu-Med—also went through bankruptcy reorganization.
- Republic Health Corporation—went through bankruptcy reorganization, became OrNda Health Corporation, then sold to Tenet.
- Summit Health—bought by OrNda in 1994.
- Universal Health Services—still around with the same top management. Has made some strategic acquisitions in 1996 and 1997 and was the best performing hospital stock of 1997.

So, of the companies in the preceding list, four were bought by Columbia, three went through bankruptcy reorganization, three merged with each other, and another four have had severe financial problems stemming from their psychiatric operations. Even more noteworthy is the fact that only one, Universal, remains in its current form with the same top management.

This synoptic review of the for-profit founding firms underscores a critical issue discussed throughout this book: The healthcare industry is so complex and so volatile that change is truly the only constant in the field. As mentioned earlier, the history of privately held hospital firms is either too brief or too inchoate to have merited the type of review and documentation one would expect (and hope for) from such a powerful sector of the industry. The analytical review is also disappointingly sparse when considered from the standpoint of individuals who must make critical decisions about their charitable contributions, their investments, or their personal medical care. More and more, as the face of healthcare takes on new complexity, decisions regarding the status and strategy of for-profit companies have long-term implications, but they are inherently based on short-term experience. This is one of the most perplexing dilemmas facing health industry leaders, politicians, outside interest groups, and the public, who continually query, "What is this Columbia organization all about?"

This dilemma is analogous to the literary critic who commented on the autobiography of a 30-something luminary, "I never give much credence to a biography about anyone in their thirties, because they haven't lived long enough, nor done enough, to tell you much about their true self." Those healthcare executives who want to determine the true nature of Columbia (and some of the other investor-owned healthcare firms) face a similar fate: trying to predict the future status and professional character of a relatively young firm.

The fits and starts of America's for-profit hospital companies have not been an exercise in futility, however. They've altered this industry and the way it competes. History shows that there have been plenty of mistakes, as well as examples of bad timing and considerable ambition bordering on greed. Perhaps the best example of such behavior was provided by National Medical Enterprises (NME) and its psychiatric hospitals. Under tremendous pressure to fill beds in the late 1980s, NME executives and professionals in the psychiatric hospitals purportedly paid doctors, school counselors, and other mental health workers to refer patients to them. One of NME's founders, John Bedrosian, had license plates that read "ADC," which stood for average daily census. The acronym on the license plate symbolized the focus of the firm. Administrators and others were judged (and compensated) on how many beds were full, or in hospital parlance, the census of the hospital.

What goes around comes around, though, and NME eventually paid for its questionable ethics when it settled for a record $379 million with the federal government in 1994 after a wide-ranging fraud investigation. However, NME's founders started with good intentions. "One of the joys I used to have in this business when we started the business was to know that we thought we were doing something that had a social good attached to it," Bedrosian said in a deposition taken in connection with NME's patient fraud lawsuits.

Despite these publicized transgressions, the investor-owned industry glistens with examples of courage and vision as well. Certainly that was the case with Humana and Hospital

Corporation of America, which pushed the boundaries of hospital operations into new frontiers. Both companies rose to prominence, taking on new challenges that eventually proved to be too soon, too grand, and, perhaps, even too self-serving. After all, this is a heady business. Even the smallest hospital chain amounts to a multimillion-dollar business. Even the smallest hospital deals in human lives. Put that on a grand scale, and one realizes that this industry cannot be compared to any other.

Not only is healthcare one of the nation's biggest businesses, it's also one of the most prestigious. The world beats a path to our hospitals. Humana founder, David Jones, used to say, "Get me an American who's sick in Germany and the first words out of his mouth are going to be, 'I want to go home.'" It's no coincidence that Humana, after it had been emulated for its financial skills, aimed to become a world leader in medicine with the artificial heart transplants in 1984. It could have been the company's zenith. Instead, it began a series of missteps that led to Humana's multimillion-dollar losses and the company's dismantling.

Still, Humana's David Jones and HCA's Thomas Frist Jr., M.D., have been hailed as visionaries. Unfortunately, vision sometimes clashes with reality for companies whose fate is in the hands of the stock market. When growth is dictated by shareholder value (getting a higher price for the company's stock), vision may be compromised by the discipline required to produce quarterly earnings gains. Once a company is owned by shareholders, it puts certain financial formulas into motion: return on equity, earnings per share, and price/earnings ratios. The wheels start cranking on a moving sidewalk toward bigger and bigger profits. Stop the sidewalk and stockholders will abandon you in droves.

IN THE BEGINNING, THERE WAS MEDICARE . . .

What started the industry's gears into motion in the first place? Arguably, it was Medicare. Introduced as part of President

Lyndon Johnson's own vision of a great society, Medicare paid hospitals and physicians to treat the elderly. It also became one of many taxpayer-supported programs developed by the Johnson administration that made Americans more dependent on government. In the case of healthcare, Medicare became the single largest customer for doctors and hospitals. It proved to be a great arrangement for hospitals. Essentially, the federal government gave hospitals a blank check: Just add up your costs, fill in the blanks, and Uncle Sam will reimburse you. The more you spend, the more you get paid.

"You couldn't lose money," said Nashville businessman Joel Gordon of those palmy days of Medicare. A cash-flow spigot was turned on, and hospital use by Americans over age 65 quadrupled within four years of the program's introduction. The country suddenly needed more and more hospitals. Gordon started a nursing home company, General Care Corporation, in 1969 in Nashville, but quickly switched to hospitals when a group of doctors urged him to convert a 250-bed nursing home into one. Gordon realized the idea was sound, and soon he and his team traveled the countryside, meeting with doctors who wanted to build hospitals. General Care would hold a 51 percent interest in the new hospital; the doctors would take 49 percent.

On the West Coast, Uranus "Bob" Appel formed American Medical International from a laboratory company he started in 1956. A microbiologist by training, he bought his first two hospitals in 1960 and raised a whopping $180,000 in the company's initial public offering.

Up until the 1960s, hospitals primarily were owned by either churches (like the Catholics, Methodists, and Baptists) or community-sponsored organizations—with a 501(c)3 (the IRS classification for a not-for-profit, tax exempt institution) designation. Some doctors owned hospitals as well, but there were no hospital companies. Chains were okay for fast-food restaurants and department stores, but not for hospitals.

When the Federation of American Hospitals (a splinter group that represents only for-profit hospitals) formed in 1966, nearly all of its members were doctors. Yet, others were seeing the financial potential provided by Medicare, and corporate chains began popping up throughout the country, especially in the southeast. The industry's not-for-profit majority didn't appreciate the arrival of these newcomers, however.

THE INVESTOR-OWNED SECTOR IS BORN

A hospital developer from Portland, Oregon, Eugene Brim, was one of the Federation's founders who grappled with ill will from not-for-profit hospitals. "There was such antagonism from not-for-profits who labeled the corporate hospital owners as 'proprietary,'" said Brim.

Brim and others didn't like that name. At an early meeting of Federation members, "I said, 'what about investor-owned?'" Brim recalled. With that, a moniker was born. In 1969, Michael Bromberg was hired as the Federation's executive director and the complexion of the organization, now called the Federation of American Health Systems (FAHS), started to change. "I remember our board switched overnight almost from doctors to businessmen," Bromberg said. By 1970, several chains had formed: American Medical International (the first for-profit hospital chain), National Medical Enterprises, Hospital Corporation of America, and Humana.

HCA—THE PATRIARCH OF FOR-PROFIT HOSPITALS

Tommy Frist Jr. was a 28-year-old Air Force flight surgeon with time on his hands to think while stationed in Georgia during the early 1960s. He knew of Kemmons Wilson, who started a chain of hotels called Holiday Inns. The young doctor began to think of the 5,000-plus hospitals in America and how they might be similarly linked.

"I just plagiarized the concept," he explained. He returned to Nashville and talked to his dad, Thomas Frist Sr., who coincidentally needed to find a buyer for Park View Hospital, a Nashville hospital that he had helped found in 1960. Father and son linked up with two other key men: the late Jack Massey, who created a $500 million empire known as Kentucky Fried Chicken (KFC) and Henry Hooker, a founder of the lesser-known enterprise, Minnie Pearl's Chicken. Together, they started the company, in which each of the four held equal shares.

Six months later, Hooker dropped out, but Massey was in for good. Three years after starting HCA with Frist, Massey, who was credited with creating the fast-food industry, resigned as KFC's chairman to concentrate on a new horizon as chairman of HCA. In a May 30, 1970, article in *Business Week,* Massey said that selling fried chicken and running hospitals had a lot in common: "The secret is in the management."

Not-for-profit hospital executives scoffed at these upstarts. Calling Massey and HCA "chicken pluckers," John R. Gadd, a director of Lee Memorial Hospital in Fort Myers, Florida, told *Business Week* that the for-profits were only providing the services with high profit margins, ignoring obstetrics and emergency rooms. How irrelevant that argument seems today. With many investor-owned hospitals in the suburbs, obstetrics is an essential service for young families. As for emergency rooms, these days, not many hospitals can get licensed without one.

HCA went public in 1969, selling 400,000 shares. The stock was an instant hit. On the first day of trading, HCA stock jumped from $18 to $46 per share. Success breeds copycats. By 1971, there were thirty-eight investor-owned hospital chains, more than a dozen of which were traded on the major stock exchanges.

The hospital corporate chains were quick to attract attention. An article in the November, 1974 *Harvard Business Review* noted the criticism of investor-owned chains: "cream-skimmers" who take only the highest-paying patients. Similar charges (of skimming the cream) have been made against competitors in other regulated industries, such as the postal service and the telephone systems, the article pointed out. "The charge that profit-making hospitals are less costly because they cut too many corners seems hard to reconcile with another charge—that they

cater only to affluent patients. Why would affluent patients settle for inadequate services?" the article questioned.

During the next few years, HCA built hospitals. Most were
in the South, to which the population was migrating but often
didn't have the money to build their own hospitals. Often, those
cities didn't want to turn to a for-profit company, but they didn't
have any other choice. Many community hospitals had been
built with funds through the Hill-Burton Act, a 1946 initiative
in which Congress administered funds to build hospitals. By the
1960s, those funds had ebbed, and hospital corporations such as
HCA stepped in to finance the South's new hospitals.

The government, in fact, was doing little to encourage the
industry. In 1973, President Nixon proposed a broad healthcare
cost containment effort. The legislation that passed endorsed a
new concept called health maintenance organizations (HMOs).
The new concept didn't exactly capture consumers' fancies. In
the first ten years of its existence, the HMO option was selected
by less than five percent of the population. However, after a
quarter of a century, HMOs have enrollment of approximately
25 percent of the U.S. population and have emerged as a domi-
nant player in the healthcare industry.

Government policy continued to make the hospital industry's future look dim. In 1977, Health Education and Welfare
(HEW) Secretary Joseph Califano proposed decertifying 100,000
inpatient beds so that hospitals had to maintain a minimum
85 percent occupancy rate. President Carter proposed the
Hospital Cost Containment Act of 1977, calling for a nine percent cap on hospital revenue increases. Wall Street worried
whether such measures might hinder the revenue growth of
hospital chains (point of reference: a one-day hospital stay in
1977 cost $158). On the economic front, interest rates were
brimming and would hit 16 percent by 1979.

HCA GOES ON THE ACQUISITION TRAIL

Fortunately for the industry, the Carter administration's proposals went nowhere, and soon Frist was on the acquisition trail.

Massey had set a goal of having 100 hospitals in 10 years, and he was determined to meet it. In 1978, he recruited Donald MacNaughton, who had been Prudential Insurance Corporation's CEO since 1969. He was one of America's most recognized CEOs, but at the age of 61 had decided to pass the post on to the next guy and look for another job.

Massey called, thinking MacNaughton would give the younger Frist and his colleagues some seasoned management combined with large corporate experience. After all, MacNaughton had traded managing Prudential's $46 billion in assets for HCA's much smaller $707 million.

In 1980, HCA bought Gordon's General Care, a 12-hospital chain, for $78 million and then followed in 1981 with the acquisition of Hospital Affiliates, HCA's hometown competitor, for $950 million. A Nashville-based firm that owned or leased 57 hospitals and managed another 102 facilities, Hospital Affiliates jump-started HCA's climb to the top.

Good timing was a cornerstone of the Hospital Affiliates deal. At a March 25, 1981, board meeting, INA, a Philadelphia-based insurer, had already decided to sell Hospital Affiliates. Two days later, MacNaughton called and offered to buy it, not knowing that INA had decided to sell. Within weeks, the deal was done.

MacNaughton's good fortune in snagging Hospital Affiliates also indirectly jump-started a healthcare economic development boom in Nashville, as several executives from Hospital Affiliates went on to start their own companies. Just as Federal Express recharged Memphis, and General Motors built Detroit, HCA created an industry for Nashville beyond the wailing steel guitars of country music.

HCA built fortunes for its executives and their families; it nurtured entrepreneurs who would start some 20 publicly held healthcare companies, including PhyCor, Allied Clinical Labs, Hospital Management Professionals, and Coventry Corporation. All of this healthcare spawning and subdividing occurred alongside not-for-profit powerhouses such as Baptist and St. Thomas hospitals in a city of a half-million residents.

Investor-owned healthcare executives created their own clique that encouraged entrepreneurial ideas. PhyCor, for example, was formed by 10-year HCA veteran Joseph Hutts. PhyCor actually created another investor-owned healthcare industry that is blossoming: ownership and management of physician groups.

Hospital Affiliates executives formed two other hospital chains: Republic Health Corporation, which went through a series of financial restructurings before emerging as OrNda Health Corporation, and Community Health Systems, a Houston-based hospital chain that found success managing rural and suburban hospitals. Another spawn was Medical Care America, a Dallas-based firm, led by former Hospital Affiliates executive Don Steen and purchased by Columbia for $860 million in 1994.

Nashville became a laboratory for healthcare companies whose executives had learned the ropes at HCA (see Figure 1–1). It was like having a corporate mentor as a neighbor. Financing was also available. Third National Bank funded HCA, Hospital Affiliates, and General Care in Nashville as well as Humana in Louisville. Third National's former chairman, Charles Kane, served on HCA's board. Those companies "offered an opportunity to add a little more business management to the healthcare industry," Kane said. Massey's company, Massey Burch Investment Group, still operates in Nashville, providing venture capital funding to young healthcare companies.

HCA "served as a model to people who had entrepreneurial spirit. They'd say, 'They're no smarter than I am; I can do that too,'" said Surgical Care's Gordon. HCA helped Gordon finance an outpatient surgery center chain. With $2 million from HCA and a $6 million line of credit, Gordon formed Surgical Care Affiliates, a highly successful independent surgery center chain, which was eventually purchased by HealthSouth Corporation, the giant rehabilitation company out of Birmingham, Alabama.

In the 1980s, HCA was a builder with Tommy Frist Jr. as its architect. By that time, Thomas Frist Sr. had turned the reins over to his son. Although not-for-profit hospitals often discounted this "offshoot" of the industry, HCA attracted talented executives who believed in the Frist's determination and ethics. "They really ran the business like you were taught in Sunday

Nashville's Health Care Family Tree

Hospital Affiliates Inc. was purchased by HCA in 1981

Hospital Corporation of America

Founders

Dr. Thomas Frist Sr
Dr. Thomas Frist Jr
Jack Massey
Henry Hooker
Gene Kidd

Spinoffs

Healthtrust Inc
(Clayton McWhorter)
Allied Clinical Labs
(Haywood Cochrane)
Quorum Health
(Jim Dalton)

Headed or founded by former HCA officials

Cumberland Health Systems

Rivendell

PhyCor

Surgical Care Affiliates

Wessex
(Bought by Diversicare)
Equicor
(Bought by Cigna Corp)

Financing

Massey Burch Investment Group
(Jack Massey)
Has provided financing for
Surgical Care Affiliates
PhyCor
Inforum

Hospital Affiliates Inc.

Founders

Baron Coleman
Irwin Eskind
Richard Eskind
Herbert Schulman

Spinoffs

Hospital Affiliates Development Corp.
(Ken Burress, O.B. McCoin)

Headed or founded by former Hospital Affiliates Inc. officials

American HealthCorp.

National Rehabilitation Centers

Coventry Corp.

Skilled Care Corp.

Hospital Management Professionals

CareNet

PhyCor

Community Health Systems

Affiliates Group

Health Horizons, Inc.

Figure 1–1.

Source: *Nashville Banner*

school," said Stanton Tuttle, who joined HCA in 1980 and was one of its top three executives before leaving in 1986. "Whatever you told anybody verbally, you'd honor." Executives didn't have written contracts because they knew Tommy Frist was good for his word. "They treated people right," Tuttle said.

HCA PURSUES A NOT-FOR-PROFIT HOSPITAL

By the early 1980s, Frist was getting positive feedback about his investor-owned company. "We had proven we could be responsible corporate citizens," he said. It was time for some big moves. Those moves soon came knocking at the door of not-for-profit healthcare. Frist initiated a move that became a disturbing wake-up call to his not-for-profit competitors. It was akin to David Letterman moving from NBC to CBS or Wayne Gretzky leaving Canada to play hockey for a U.S. team.

The board of Wesley Medical Center, a 760-bed teaching hospital in Wichita, Kansas, agreed to sell the not-for-profit hospital to HCA for $265 million in late 1984. The buyout stunned administrators at not-for-profit hospitals, especially those who belonged to Voluntary Hospitals of America (VHA), a growing not-for-profit alliance that Wesley's former CEO, Roy House, helped found.

Just three years earlier, VHA's new CEO Don Arnwine had been featured on the cover of *Modern Healthcare* with the headline: "VHA: Can volunteerism stop the investor-owned companies?" Not-for-profit hospitals hoped so. They were buying shares in the alliance and combining their purchasing clout to get vendor discounts on everything from intravenous pumps to surgical supplies. After all, VHA's member CEOs ran large not-for-profit hospitals and wanted some of the same advantages as investor-owned chains. Clearly, VHA was designed to help hospitals such as Wesley compete with for-profit hospitals such as HCA. HCA's purchase of Wesley was viewed as caving in to the "enemy."

Unlike today, when many hospital CEOs follow a career ladder that sometimes bounces between investor-owned and not-for-profit hospitals, back in the early days of investor-owned chains, administrators only worked one side of the tax-status street. Predictably, investor-owned hospitals were considered adversaries. What's more, no one expected investor-owned chains to just waltz in and buy large, prestigious, not-for-profit medical centers. Trustees wouldn't take the time to listen to the sales pitch. Instead, for-profit chains stuck to building their own hospitals or scooping up financially struggling institutions. Consequently, the Wesley sale was a bolt from the blue.

"It was one of the biggest 'why's' of my life," said Don Arnwine, the former VHA president, now a private consultant. Arnwine remembers that the only answer he received came from the hospital's CEO, A.B. "Jack" Davis, who told Arnwine that he saw "storm clouds on the horizon." Congress was debating cutbacks in reimbursement, and utilization was forecast to drop—not unlike the dire predictions that circle the industry today. "In retrospect, the storm clouds people are seeing today are much, much darker," Arnwine said, adding, "It still remains a giant puzzle to me."

In those days, hospital acquisitions were typically valued on a dollar-per-bed calculation, and the Wesley buy was a staggering $348,684 per bed. Arnwine pointed out that even today, few institutions of Wesley's reputation have been scooped up by for-profit chains. (In 1994, Columbia agreed to merge its Atlanta hospitals with Emory University, a highly regarded healthcare system. However, that deal eventually imploded, in part because Emory heard negative feedback from several smaller Georgia hospitals from which it received referrals. Subsequently, Columbia was able to enter into joint ventures with not-for-profit facilities or systems with outstanding reputations, such as Tulane University Medical Center in New Orleans and Methodist Healthcare System in San Antonio.)

The Wesley deal stirred passions. Roy House, who had been Wesley's CEO for 24 years before retiring in 1981, returned to Wichita to try to convince the board not to do the HCA deal. "Roy had spent virtually his entire career and was personally invested in that place in a way few people are today," Arnwine said. "He had taken it from a little 20-bed hospital to the pre-eminent institution in that part of the country."

Even so, the die was cast. Although some Methodist officials initially balked at the deal, they were assuaged by a reported $32 million from sale proceeds that would be used to fund a new foundation. A trend was starting, and the Wesley announcement was followed by another blockbuster sale of a not-for-profit hospital. In March 1985, Presbyterian–St. Luke's Medical Center in Denver agreed to be sold to American Medical International (AMI) in Beverly Hills for $178 million. HCA also had bid for Presbyterian but lost out to AMI. Nonetheless, HCA gobbled up other large not-for-profit hospitals in Oklahoma, Utah, and New Mexico.

For example, in February 1985, HCA purchased 80 percent of Lovelace Medical Center, in Albuquerque, New Mexico, which was among the best positioned facilities in the industry for the coming wave of managed care. Lovelace also operated a group practice clinic, like The Mayo Clinic in Rochester, Minnesota, or The Ochsner Clinic in New Orleans. The advantage of such structures lies in the incentive arrangement, under which both the hospital and the doctors are financially aligned in the same organization.

Amazingly, in less than one year, HCA purchased more than $1 billion in not-for-profit hospitals. Frist recalled that many advisers told him not to buy teaching hospitals such as Wesley. "Those were some of the best decisions we ever made," he countered. "It took us to a new level." Critics who charged that HCA wasn't interested in teaching, research, and charity could only scratch their heads at HCA's new acquisitions. However, the biggest bombshell was still to come.

HCA AND AMERICAN HOSPITAL SUPPLY

On April Fool's Day, 1985, HCA and the American Hospital Supply Corporation (American) announced that they would merge into a vertically integrated healthcare company, an

$8.5 billion corporation. Frist and American's CEO, the late Karl Bays, explained to a stunned industry that the merger was a way for both companies to save money and expand. A giant manufacturer and distributor of all kinds of hospital supplies, American could be folded into the HCA corporate structure, cutting a wide swath through HCA's purchasing costs. Together, the merged companies (to be called Kuron) could borrow as much as $1 billion to buy more hospitals, more HMOs, and more pharmaceutical manufacturers, or so Frist and Bays reasoned.

By this time, HCA was a powerhouse, owning or managing 366 acute-care hospitals with 54,324 beds, 28 psychiatric hospitals with 3,619 beds, and 27 foreign hospitals with 2,722 beds. It also owned 17 percent of Beverly Enterprises, the nation's largest nursing home chain. Because of its size, HCA was beginning to feel boxed in. Investor-owned chains were still located primarily in the South, and the company was risking antitrust problems if it expanded too much. Frist knew the company had to keep growing, but the question was, how? "I thought about putting together a GE (General Electric) of healthcare," he explained. "At that time, GE owned Kidder Peabody and other lines of business."

Yet, some of Frist's own men were telling him the merger with American could backfire. Not-for-profit hospitals were starting to decry HCA, and they would surely not do anything that would fatten its coffers. Frist's executives knew this, warning him that American's other hospital customers would abandon the company once it became a part of HCA. Large purchasing groups of not-for-profit hospitals, such as VHA and the Daughters of Charity, the nation's largest Catholic hospital system based in St. Louis, Missouri, could pull as much as $500 million in American Hospital Supply's business.

Despite the warnings from inside their own companies, Frist and Bays pressed ahead. HCA signed a five-year lease in a Nashville office building for the proposed company (Kuron), sure that the deal would go through. "There was so much underlying value," Frist explained. "I had an exit strategy."

Frist figured he could sell the distribution business or the manufacturing business if things didn't work out. Bays himself was talking to Arnwine about VHA buying the company's distribution business. VHA was an alliance of large not-for-profit hospitals that had started a purchasing program with Bays' help. Bays and Arnwine became personal friends, and Bays pleaded with Arnwine to keep the alliance's business.

Almost immediately after the announcement, both companies' worst fears were realized. VHA, Daughters of Charity, and Humana gave American 60 days' notice. They were threatening to pull their business. Even worse, Wall Street revolted. HCA and American stocks both dropped more than $2.50 a share. "How would this deal fill hospital beds?" one Wall Street analyst questioned. Many saw the move merely as a grab for growth, and an ill-advised one at that. However, American's mate for life was waiting in the wings. Baxter Travenol (now Baxter International), another Chicago-area hospital supply firm, swept in with a hostile offer. American rejected the offer, and an irate HCA canceled its $40 million intravenous supply contract with Baxter in retaliation for the hostile interference. HCA raised its offer, but Baxter upped its ante to $53 a share for a total price of $3.6 billion.

Inexplicably, HCA folded its cards in retreat. With HCA pulling out, Bays's great vision melted away. "Bays said he felt like Tommy Frist left him in the middle of Lake Michigan without any oars," commented one source about HCA's decision not to outbid Baxter. Yet, Frist answered: "It only made sense to go down that path if you paid the right amount." In the end, Bays would become chairman of Baxter, but leave the healthcare industry 18 months later to head IC Industries, a Chicago-based conglomerate.

Actually, HCA emerged from the battle in strong financial shape. It withdrew its bid, taking a $150 million payoff for its trouble. In addition, HCA was promised another $50 million in 1991 if it bought more than $1.325 billion in supplies over the next five years.

HCA HEALTH PLANS: THE START OF A DOWNWARD SLIDE

HCA then decided to follow the lead of Humana, diving into the insurance business. With a bravado that was becoming characteristic, HCA announced that it was launching HCA Health Plans in the summer of 1985.

Company officials said they expected to have one million subscribers by December 1987 and insurance revenues of $1 billion by 1988. The plan was for HCA to offer a host of health plans, not just an HMO. To get started, the chain bought a Los Angeles HMO with 16,000 members for $24 million. Company officials said they planned to spend another $125 million to buy other health plans in 1985.

For a while, the future looked rosy. A consultant's strategic report to top HCA executives in 1986 predicted that HCA would be an $11 billion company by 1992. That forecast never materialized. In the second quarter, ending June 30, 1985, HCA reported a 26 percent drop in profits to $67 million. Frist blamed a $7.2 million loss in its health plan business and said that hospital occupancy had dropped to 48 percent. Patient days were down 2.3 percent compared to the previous year.

Things didn't look as though they were going to get better soon. The Reagan administration had just proposed a thin, half-percent increase in Medicare rates for 1987. Much of the industry entered a slump. Republic Health Corporation, started by former Hospital Affiliates executives, mortgaged itself to the hilt with a management-led leveraged buyout (LBO) in the fall of 1986 and immediately hit a financial wall.

Republic had purchased eighteen money-losing hospitals from HCA for $215 million and had managed to turn them around. However, the magic didn't last. The LBO was more than the company could bear. With more than $800 million in high-yield debt, Republic soon began gagging on its $25 million in quarterly interest payments. It was losing $2 million a week on operations and began a frantic search for buyers for its hospitals.

The trouble was that the now-slumping industry was full of distressed properties. Republic's hospitals were only one-third full, and insiders soon realized the company's debt exceeded the value of its assets. Analysts valued Republic's hospitals at about $600 million. In other words, even if the company found a buyer, it still couldn't pay off the debt. Republic wasn't the only hospital chain in trouble. American Healthcare Management (AHM), another Dallas-based chain, began having cash-flow troubles and was forced into Chapter 11 bankruptcy reorganization in the fall of 1987. Amid a vicious battle with its banks, the company finally emerged from bankruptcy two years later.

AHM's top executives, like many of their cohorts, blamed Medicare's new diagnosis-related group (DRG) system (which paid hospitals a fixed amount based on a patient's diagnosis) rather than their own missteps. AHM's executives didn't survive the bankruptcy reorganization.

In 1987, only half of the nation's hospitals made a profit on patient operations, according to HCIA, a Baltimore research firm that specializes in hospital financial information. Medicare margins had been in the 14 percent range in 1984. As a result of DRGs, the margins dropped to 5 percent by 1987, according to the Health Care Financing Administration (HCFA), the government agency that oversees Medicare.

"A lot of the companies during the 1980s argued that a lot of their problems were related to DRGs," said Steve Volla, who was brought in to turn around AHM. After righting the ship at AHM, he engineered a merger with OrNda Health Corporation, a Nashville-based hospital chain, in 1984. (Volla eventually started another hospital company, Primary Health Systems.) "Yet, DRGs in the 1980s were an easy scapegoat. It showed that some companies weren't ready." Volla recently noted, "We're still with the same DRG system, and the for-profits still are handsomely surviving."

HCA PARES DOWN TO THE CORE

Size didn't necessarily insulate America's largest hospital chain, HCA. What happened to HCA is often viewed as an example of what could happen to its descendent, Columbia/HCA. By 1987, HCA owned 225 U.S. hospitals and 25 foreign hospitals, and had management contracts to operate another 200 hospitals. Still, Frist was forced to dismantle the empire in the name of shareholder value.

First, he streamlined costs, taking $125 million in annual corporate overhead and cutting it to $28 million. Then, the divestitures began. On August 31, 1987, he spun off 104 hospitals—widely regarded as "the marginal performers"—to HealthTrust in a $2.1 billion deal. Of course, HCA kept its jewel, Wesley in Wichita, a 760-bed lion with a strong 71 percent occupancy.

Although the Healthtrust spin-off positioned HCA as a stronger company, it didn't help the stock price. To boost shareholder value, HCA proposed buying back 12 million shares at $47 per share in September. Then came the October 1987 stock market crash, which hammered HCA shares down to $30. To make matters worse, the financial windfall from selling hospitals to HealthTrust didn't look like such a great success on the books. Although HCA recorded a $300 million gain on the sale of HealthTrust, the Securities and Exchange Commission (SEC) said it had to defer the profit to future periods. The result was that HCA was forced to pay taxes on the gain of $140 million. That resulted in a $58 million loss in 1987.

The stock buyback at $47 per share paid shareholders a premium, yet HCA stock continued to languish with share values in the low- to mid-30s through much of 1988. Fearing a takeover of the family-started business, Frist (in September 1988) proposed a leveraged buyout to take HCA private at $51 per share. Going private would also take HCA (whose stability was at the opposite extreme of other investor-owned hospital firms such as AMI) off the market for takeovers.

In what would prove to be an interesting harbinger, in 1987 Frist and his board had rebuffed an out-of-the-blue offer from two former Republic Health executives and their attorney, Richard Scott. That incident would provide the backdrop for Scott's remarkable rise in the hospital industry. (Several months later, Scott founded Columbia Hospital Corporation with Fort

Worth, Texas, financial whiz Richard Rainwater). "I didn't even
know who he was," Frist said about Scott. "That's how ridiculous
the era was. He had $25,000 in his pocket, and he was offering
to buy a $5 billion company." Frist realized that if an unknown
like Rick Scott could marshal enough junk bond capital to take
over his company, he'd better do something.

Takeover fever had gripped Wall Street, which at the time
was atwitter with the celebrated bidding war for RJR Nabisco.
That $25-billion megadeal for the cigarette and cookie giant later
spawned a book and movie, *Barbarians at the Gate,* about the "in-
sanity" surrounding Wall Street's wheeler-dealers. HCA's deal—
the largest LBO in the history of the hospital industry—would appear small by comparison, but prove vastly more successful than
the much ballyhooed RJR transaction. Kohlberg Kravis Roberts &
Co. (KKR), won the bidding in history's largest LBO ever.

Notably, KKR, considering a counteroffer for HCA, had
looked at the company's books after Frist and his managers
made a bid for the company. Intent on winning RJR, KKR partner Henry Kravis diverted his attention away from HCA.
Ironically, RJR Chairman Ross Johnson eventually lost his company to KKR. Tommy Frist did not lose his firm.

Amid talks that Humana might make an offer, Frist and his
managers ended up being the only bidders for HCA, which became a private company once again in March 1989. KKR's deal
for RJR Nabisco closed within a week of HCA's. Frist saw Kravis
a week after that. The HCA founder congratulated the Wall
Street baron for winning RJR, then asked him why he hadn't
pursued HCA. "Tommy," Kravis said, "I understand Oreo cookies
better than I do DRGs."

HCA's LBO burdened the hospital company with a staggering $4.5 billion in debt. However, none of it was high-yield junk
bond debt. Frist himself pledged 100 percent of net worth, and
twenty-one officers of HCA pledged half of their net worth to get
the loans. The company was 90 percent leveraged and its debt
was costing $85,000 an hour, Frist recalled.

Radical surgery had to be done to pare down costs and sell
assets so that HCA could begin to repay its debt. The company's

contract management group was sold to senior managers and Welsh Carson Anderson & Stowe, a New York–based venture capital firm, for $44 million. Renamed Quorum Health Group and led by longtime HCA executive, James Dalton, Quorum emerged as a hospital chain in its own right.

Frist also sold the company's British and Australian hospitals and was poised to sell a highly valued asset: the psychiatric business. Over the preceding few years, HCA had built the nation's largest chain of freestanding psychiatric hospitals, with 6,000 beds. The psychiatric division had the highest operating margins and the fastest growth in HCA. While medical-surgical hospitals were struggling, the psychiatric facilities were prospering.

The math worked out perfectly. The psychiatric hospitals were to be sold for $1.6 billion. HCA would then take the proceeds to repay a $1.3-billion bridge loan taken out to finance the LBO. Frist's idea was to sell the mental health business to its employees, the same way it had with Healthtrust. Employee stock ownership plans (ESOPs) were a hot trend. AMI had orchestrated a similar arrangement, selling its less profitable hospitals to an ESOP, Epic Healthcare Group, in 1988.

Nonetheless, the deal was a struggle from day one. Starting in March 1989, Jim Don, president of the psychiatric company, and Vic Campbell, HCA's vice president of investor relations, took the proposed arrangement to New York, visiting with high-level executives from Chase Manhattan, Bankers Trust, Citicorp, and Bank of Nova Scotia.

After the presentations, the bankers cornered Don. "What do you really think?" they asked. Don was in a precarious position. On one hand he was representing a new company that would have to pay off a $1-billion-plus loan. On the other hand, he was a long-time HCA executive, loyal to Frist and the company. "I was kind of caught in the middle," Don said later.

In the July 24, 1989, issue of *Forbes,* the questionable economics of the deal hit the fan. The article, headlined "A crazy deal?", charged that Frist was forcing his employees to pay "through the nose" for the psychiatric business. The magazine also suggested that the U.S. Labor Department (the watchdog of ESOPs) should look into HCA's proposal.

Weeks passed. The industry was changing quickly, and not for the better. Though few could have predicted it at the time, the psychiatric inpatient business was within a year of going into a deep and dangerous tailspin, motored by overbuilding and greed. The overbuilding would bring aggressive advertising campaigns and tactics that would turn the industry into a financial nightmare.

By late 1989, negative news stories began sprouting about the inappropriate hospitalization of teenagers. That, coupled with uncertainty about the proposed spin-off, began to affect HCA's psychiatric hospitals. Physicians and employees were recruited away in what had become a fiercely competitive field. All of the psychiatric hospitals were pressured to fill their beds amid a glut of capacity and increasingly reluctant payors. As the deal lingered, the price dropped. By September 1989, the price tag was down to $1.1 billion, and Frist decided to shop the company around to outside bidders.

Thirty bids came in, including offers by Charter Medical Corporation, the second largest psychiatric hospital chain, and two investment banking firms, First Boston Corporation and Morgan Stanley. Charter had just finished a $1.4 billion LBO by management, which eventually jackknifed the Macon, Georgia–based chain into bankruptcy. Given their eventual problems, one can only imagine what would have happened had Charter swallowed the $1 billion buy of HCA's psychiatric hospitals.

In the meantime, Don and his managers put an equity and junk bond financing package together with Kidder Peabody (another New York–based investment banking firm), Bank of Nova Scotia, and General Electric Capital Credit to buy the HCA hospitals. Then, in October the bottom fell out of the junk bond market, sending HCA back to the drawing board. Next, Don and his team put together a proposal to split up the hospitals: forty-seven would be put in the new company, while the other eight to ten marginal performers would be sold at their real estate value. Still, the price dropped, and the deal lingered, undone.

Finally, in December a savior stepped in. Cigna Corporation, out of Philadelphia, offered to buy HCA's 50 percent stake in its insurance subsidiary, Equicor, for $777 million in cash. Equicor had been a joint venture between HCA and Equitable Life Assurance Society, out of New York. With these developments, the pressure was off. Frist could repay the bridge loan with the proceeds and cash from a $545 million recapitalization. He didn't have to sell the psychiatric business. Jim Don left the same month to start American Day Treatment Centers, a chain of day treatment centers for mental healthcare. That company, based in Baltimore, marketed itself to payors as a cost-efficient alternative to inpatient psychiatric treatment.

Ironically, HCA ended up selling or closing at least half of its psychiatric hospitals, as the mental health business took a nosedive under clouds of scandal in the early 1990s. Out from under the Equicor arrangement and the bridge loan repayment, HCA forged ahead, striving to focus once again on acute-care hospitals. "We alienated three physicians for every one we pleased," Frist told *Modern Healthcare* (January 2, 1987) in explaining the company's exit from managed care. Nearly everyone started exiting the managed care field. Everyone, that is, except Humana.

HUMANA CORPORATION STRIVES TO BE THE INDUSTRY LEADER

As much as Thomas Frist Jr. was regarded as an empire builder, Humana's top executives, David Jones and the late Wendell Cherry, were visionaries tempered by business-school priorities. Followers of management guru Peter Drucker, Jones and Cherry studied the ways of IBM and Xerox and molded Humana into a hospital-chain version of those businesses.

Humana provided the investor-owned industry with lessons in centralization. For example, hospital administrators had to deposit their daily receipts by 3 P.M. Those deposits were then reinvested by Humana's financial leaders by 5 P.M. Humana executives realized the power of the cash flow that the healthcare industry could generate.

Jones and Cherry took the hospital industry in new directions, never happy with the status quo. "It was addicting working there because you knew you were going to learn so much in the next six months," said a former employee.

These men (two Louisville attorneys) were as close as two business associates could be. Cherry was a sounding board for Jones's ideas and vice versa. Humana was started in 1961 as a nursing home business, Extendicare. Jones, Cherry, and four other investors each put up $1,000 to get it started. Cherry found the nursing home business depressing, however, and in 1968, the company switched to hospitals. After soliciting professional advice, the company's name was changed to Humana.

In January 1968, Jones and Cherry took the Louisville company public at $8 a share. Within 10 months, the price had soared to $50 a share, and the two founders were instant millionaires. Unlike General Care and some of the other hospital chains, Humana didn't enter the joint-venture spree with physicians. "He [Jones] believed there was a fundamental conflict between doctors and hospitals, and where that existed, it was best not to mix money," said Ira Korman, a former Humana hospital administrator.

HUMANA BECOMES A SHARK

In the early 1970s, Humana grew extensively. Then in 1978, Jones's ambition turned gritty, a characteristic loved by Wall Street. Jones made an unfriendly bid for a much larger company, American Medicorp, a 39-hospital chain. It was the first and last (to date) hostile hospital takeover (a stark contrast to the more agreeable deals of the 1990s).

American Medicorp had been nurtured by founders Bernard Korman and Alan Miller. The company's first purchase had been three Northwest hospitals owned by Eugene Brim and two other partners in 1968. Brim had quit American Medicorp in 1971 and had then founded his own Portland, Oregon–based company, Brim & Co., which specialized in contract management for rural hospitals. While at Medicorp, Brim signed what he maintains was the first hospital management contract with a small hospital in Coos Bay, Oregon.

American Medicorp had pursued an acquisition binge, yet its earnings didn't hold up, and its stock price fell. Humana's Jones startled Wall Street by offering $19 per share for American Medicorp stock, which was trading for $1.75. Oddly enough, Trans World Airlines (TWA), a St. Louis–based airline that lusted after the hospital chain's cash flow, upped the ante by offering $24 per share. Jones never blinked. He offered shareholders $27 a share to cinch the deal for $305 million. (Medicorp's Miller went on to found another hospital management company, Universal Health Services, which he still runs out of King of Prussia, Pennsylvania.)

The former American Medicorp hospital administrators met their new bosses for the first time at a meeting in an Indiana hotel across the river from Louisville. Fresh from the takeover victory, Humana was on a power trip. On the marquee outside the hotel were the words "Medicarp—a Dead Fish." In the hotel's tension-filled meeting room, Jones made a few things clear. "There are only two ways to do things," he told the former Medicorp executives. "The Humana way or get out."

In addition to the facility at Coos Bay, Medicorp had nine other contracts to manage hospitals that it didn't own. When an administrator from one of the managed hospitals asked Jones what his fate was to be, Jones answered bluntly, "I never understood how you can make money on managed hospitals, and we don't do what I don't understand." What Jones did understand was how to make money in the hospital business. Between 1970 and 1980, Humana's annual growth rate averaged 32 percent, which exceeded all but eight companies in *Financial World's* performance ranking for companies with revenues of more than $500 million. That same year (1980), Humana was the largest company in the hospital business with $1.4 billion in revenue.

HCA would eventually surpass Humana with the former company's expansion in the mid-1980s. Jones, however wasn't interested in sheer size. Employees often heard him say, "Being big is wonderful, but I wouldn't want an elephant to paint my house."

By 1982, an investor who had purchased 100 Humana shares at $8 per share (the initial public offering price) in January 1968 would have had 1,800 shares worth $57,375. Michael LeConey, an analyst with Merrill-Lynch at the time, called Humana the "most aggressive and smartest major company in the United States."

HUMANA AND THE ARTIFICIAL HEART

Despite such accolades from the financial community, for-profit chains lacked the high-quality reputation of some of their not-for-profit peers, such as teaching hospitals. Jones took on that challenge as well when, in 1984, he recruited William DeVries, M.D., from the University of Utah.

DeVries wasn't just any doctor, and Humana didn't have just any plans for him. DeVries was the only surgeon authorized by the Food and Drug Administration (FDA) to perform the artificial heart transplant. He had done the remarkable heart transplantation two years earlier on Barney Clark, but financial and bureaucratic hurdles prevented him from repeating the operation on another patient.

Humana rolled out the red carpet. In essence, company executives told DeVries, "We'll not only pay for you to do a second procedure in this cutting-edge technology, but we'll pay for 100." Humana pledged to donate the hospital care for as many as 100 artificial heart operations at a cost of $100,000 to $250,000 each—an investment of $25 million.

In December 1984, Dr. DeVries and his surgical team at the Humana Hospital–Audubon performed the world's second artificial implant on retired government worker William Schroeder, age 52. It was almost a carnival atmosphere in Louisville, where the Jarvik-7 heart operation established Humana as the leader in tomorrow's generation of medical wonders. The news was framed by the issue of for-profit medicine, a topic worthy of endless debate around America's dinner tables. For the first time, consumers were talking about whether profit-making corporations should control access to expensive medical procedures such as transplantation, an occurrence that only heightened media interest in the story.

The Louisville Convention Center, just five minutes away from the hospital, doubled as a press office. The event, enhanced by handout press photos of Schroeder's discarded natural heart, paid off. Not only did hundreds of newspapers pick up the story, but the surgery grabbed feature articles in the December 10, 1984, editions of *Time, Newsweek,* and *Business Week.* Even *People* magazine came calling (not the kind of publication that usually writes about hospital management types). In the December 17 edition of *People,* "high-rolling entrepreneurs" Jones and Cherry were profiled, as was Humana's new $50 million headquarters building, which was under construction in downtown Louisville. The article went on to say that critics likened the free artificial heart transplants to free samples of a new product. By giving some transplants away, other critically ill patients would see hope for their conditions in the kind of treatment that only Humana could provide.

Humana generated millions of dollars in free publicity as Americans throughout the country (regardless of whether they had a Humana hospital in their town), now knew the Humana name. Ironically, the experiment became the first in a series of stumbles for Humana. Schroeder suffered a stroke. Questions about the quality of life for these artificial patients arose, and Humana's motives were questioned. Even so, Dr. DeVries spoke of a higher calling that was consistent with Humana's rarified attitude. In an interview with *The Wall Street Journal* in 1987, Dr. DeVries rationalized the heart operations by quoting dialogue from (of all things) *The Wizard of Oz.* DeVries noted that when the Wizard told the Tinman that a heart might make him unhappy, the Tinman replied, "that must be a matter of opinion."

THE HUMANA WAY OF OPERATION

Differences of opinion were not often tolerated at Humana, however. Unlike some hospital chains in which individual hospital CEOs could establish their own budget targets, Humana's targets came down from Louisville. Executive directors at the individual hospitals had to meet specific budgets, census day volumes, and profit margins to get bonuses and stock.

Indeed, Humana hospital administrators were known as the best paid administrators in the early 1980s. Humana rewarded them well, tying bonuses and stock awards to profit margins at the individual hospitals. For example, a hospital's executive director could earn up to 50 percent of his or her salary in bonus compensation for meeting the budget, achieving established profit margins, hitting accounts receivable targets, and/or achieving targeted volumes in patient census. Interestingly, the numbers for bonus calculation were an ever-escalating target. For example, if a hospital administrator's facility made a 20 percent margin one year, Humana would raise the margin 15 percent the next year, and the amount kept going up.

By tying the bonus to profit margin goals rather than dollar profits, the company was structured to grow even during the lean times. For example, an executive director could get a $10,000 bonus for increasing census. However, he or she would receive only $5,000 at the end of the year. The other $5,000 would come in six months, if the hospital's bad debt hadn't gone up. In essence, Humana wanted to ensure that an executive director didn't pack the hospital full of patients who couldn't pay just to get his or her bonus.

To further goad executive directors, the Louisville giant established the Humana Club. Only about one-third of the company's executives earned the coveted club membership, which earned them a two-day trip to Louisville and extra stock. The first year a hospital executive director (ED) made the Humana Club, he or she received 20 percent of the cash value of his or her bonus in stock. However, Club freshmen would only get one-fifth of that stock initially; the rest would be paid over the next four years. The second year the ED made the Humana Club, he or she would receive 25 percent of the value of the bonus in stock. The same formula was used, although only one-fifth would be paid the first year. However, the ED would also get another fifth of the first year's stock award.

Each consecutive year an ED made the Humana Club, the percentage would rise by 5 percent to a cap of 55 percent. That tied an executive director to Humana and created incredible pressure to repeat at the Humana Club. One executive director called this incentive system "velvet handcuffs." There was a distinct financial penalty for jumping ship. A successful ED who quit might easily walk away from a million dollars or more. Keeping the best, most financially successful executive directors certainly served Humana's bottom line.

The formula worked. In September 1988, HCIA produced a study of the hospitals with the highest operating profit margins in 1987. Of the forty hospitals with margins of 17.5 percent or higher, seventeen (almost half) were Humana facilities. Only one of the highly profitable hospitals was a not-for-profit facility. The remaining twenty-two were investor owned. Former hospital administrator Korman likened working for Humana to playing for the legendary New York Yankees of the 1950s. As Korman stated, "Nobody liked you, but you didn't care because you knew you were the best."

Humana ran a tightly controlled ship. One example of the stringent control was found in the purchasing area. Most hospitals buy supplies through groups or cooperatives, which receive discounts because they purchase in large volumes. The more a hospital buys, the bigger the discounts. Purchasing groups sign contracts with suppliers, who promise prices based on volume. The groups, in turn, sign contracts with hospitals that commit to buy enough products to obtain the discount. For example, a hospital agrees to buy all of its sutures from Vendor A for a certain price. If the hospital buys from Vendor A, B, and C, Vendor A is going to be unhappy because it had been promised all of the business.

Non-compliance to purchasing contracts is the bane of such hospital groups. Regardless of how much the group or cooperative tries to enforce the contracts, individual hospitals often stray. Frequently, a hospital administrator wants to buy a dozen different types of sutures because each of his or her physicians has a different preference. Humana put a stop to that practice. If Humana signed a contract with one vendor for sutures, that was it. Hospital administrators were allowed to buy only those items for which the company had negotiated discounts.

In 1971, Humana believed it could lower its costs by mandating purchasing contracts. Corporate executives set a goal of 85 percent compliance from individual hospital administrators. Up to that point, compliance had been in the 25 percent range. In other words, only 25 percent of what administrators were buying were supplies on which Humana had negotiated discounts.

To further ensure that this "strongly encouraged policy" wasn't just an exercise in wishful thinking, Humana tied part of administrators' bonuses to compliance. Since Humana centralized its accounts payable function in its Louisville offices, purchasing managers could monitor the extent to which the various hospitals were buying on or off the contracts. If a hospital strayed from the policy, sometimes all it took was a phone call to get them back on the team.

In the first year, the centralized chain achieved an amazing 90 percent compliance—a powerful tool to derive even greater discounts from bandage, aspirin, and intravenous pump manufacturers. After all, a bird in the hand is worth two in the bush. With Humana, vendors had the bird in the hand: a guaranteed volume of sales. Other hospitals only offered two in the bush: more hospital members, but no discipline among the ranks to guarantee sales. Who's likely to get the best prices under that scenario? Intuitively and empirically, the answer was Humana.

This concept of centralized purchasing compliance (as we will see later in the book) is relevant in the evaluation of contemporary chains. The clout that a large healthcare system brings to the negotiating table is one of the distinguishing advantages touted by Columbia executives to achieve a cost advantage over its competition. (Centralized purchasing and purchasing compliance would eventually become hallmarks of Columbia/HCA's operating strategy.)

HUMANA'S MOVE INTO MANAGED CARE

Jones was smart. Some industry observers even called him brilliant. Importantly, he saw the tide turning. In 1979, charge-based payors made up 51 percent of Humana's revenues. That percentage was rapidly falling. Consequently, in 1983, Humana launched Humana Care Plus, the forerunner of provider-based managed care plans. Unfortunately, Care Plus was to become the company's Achilles' heel. To this day, many say that Jones and Cherry had the right idea at the wrong time.

Humana may not have had the kind of relationships with its physicians that HCA was known for, but the rapport was reasonable. It had to be. Hospitals can't treat a single patient without a physician's signature. However, its collaborative rapport with physicians was tested when Humana started tinkering with two important things: the way physicians treat patients and the way physicians are reimbursed.

Traditionally, when a patient was treated, the hospital billed the insurance company, and the physician billed the insurance company. Everybody got paid; everybody was happy. When Humana became the insurance company, and not just any insurance company, but an HMO, it decided how much the physician would get paid. In many cases, it was offering to pay them less than the physicians had typically received.

This wasn't a foolhardy experiment. The HMO concept had worked for decades for the California prototype, Kaiser Permanente. Yet, here was one big difference: Kaiser's doctors were salaried physicians, and Humana's were not. Like most physicians, Humana's physicians were free agents. There was always another hospital, another insurance company. They didn't have to put up with a company trying to make a profit at their expense.

The launch of Care Plus corresponded with another significant event in healthcare. That same year, Medicare introduced
DRGs, a prospective payment system in which hospitals were
paid a fixed amount, depending on a patient's diagnosis. This
new reimbursement arrangement put hospitals at financial
risk. The days when Medicare would pay regardless of the costs
ended abruptly. This meant patients' length of stay would drop,
because a significant percentage of hospital business (Medicare
and Medicaid) was now reimbursed on a fixed rate. The perplexing dilemma facing hospital administrators was, "Where
would the revenue from lost patient days come from?"

To survive, or better yet, thrive, hospitals needed to be at
the top of the reimbursement structure, or what was referred to
in the industry as the "food chain." In essence, hospitals needed
to be on the receiving end of the premium dollar, doling out payments to the providers, not just receiving reimbursement on a
per diem basis or getting percentage discounts off total hospital
charges.

Humana was farsighted in seeing the trend. No one was
truly "managing" the money spent on healthcare. Providers sent
in the bills and were paid, but corporate employers started com-
plaining about how the costs kept rising and rising. HMOs
promised to keep costs in check. Instead of separate charges for
the surgeon, the anesthesiologist, the hospital, the pharmacist,
and the home healthcare nurse, an employer would pay the
HMO a monthly fee for all services required. The fee would not
go up if a patient had multiple health problems that month.
Conversely, it would not go down if the patient made nary a call
to his or her physician. Corporations liked the idea of predictable premiums, but the reception by the public was luke-
warm. In 1983, HMO membership in the United States was a
sparse 12.5 million. (Ten years later, enrollment had nearly
quadrupled, and in 1997, HMO participation rose to nearly
60 million people). Consequently, Jones's vision was marred
when the changes foretold for his business didn't come nearly as
fast and comprehensively as predicted. It's one thing to set off on
a voyage with certain provisions to sustain you until you reach

your destination. Still, all the vision in the world doesn't help when the destination keeps stretching beyond your reach.

In Humana's case, timing was off by about five years. The forecasts at the time were overly optimistic in predicting market acceptance of managed care and other contemporary changes. In retrospect, brief reviews of a few of the forecasts of 1985 demonstrate how ambitious they look today. The oft-quoted Wall Street analyst Kenneth Abramowitz, of Sanford C. Bernstein & Co., predicted that fee-for-service medicine would be dead by 1990. The respected analyst also predicted that healthcare costs would drop so drastically that healthcare would make up only 9.1 percent of the gross domestic product (GDP). In fact, healthcare as a segment of the GDP continued to foment. In 1993, healthcare hit a new peak—13.6 percent of the GDP. Although the rate of increase is slowing, it shows few signs of a downward trend.

Abramowitz also predicted major price wars among hospitals by 1987. That, too, did not occur. Based on such predictions and the market momentum that Humana seemed to possess, coupled with the fact that Jones seemed so certain at the time, most of the big chains followed in his misguided footsteps. It's often said that the hospital industry has a herd mentality. One could offer a textbook case for that thesis with the Humana foray into managed care. By 1985, HCA and AMI had acquired insurance companies, and NME was shopping for one.

THE INFLUENCE OF INVESTOR-OWNED HOSPITALS ON NOT-FOR-PROFIT HOSPITALS

Not wanting to be left behind, the not-for-profit hospitals joined the parade in getting into the insurance business. In 1983 (the same year Humana launched its Care Plus managed care product), VHA, the nation's largest alliance with 700 not-for-profit hospitals, launched VHA Enterprises (VHAE). Designed to eventually tap the stock market, VHAE dove into several ventures. Fueled by what its executives thought might be an unending source of capital from not-for-profit hospitals, VHAE started individual companies in home healthcare, mobile imaging, physician search, chemical dependency treatment, medical office buildings, long-term care, and market information. However, its most expensive venture (and eventually Enterprises' downfall) was Partners Health Plans, a 50–50 joint venture with Aetna Life & Casualty Co., a Hartford, Connecticut–based insurer.

VHAE executives were probably correct when they envisioned managed care as the wave of the future. However, they were not as accurate about other things. For example, VHAE's chief architect, Thomas Reed, vastly underestimated the financial patience required. "They completely underestimated the amount of time, resources, skills, and personnel it would take to cultivate individual markets," said Sharon Graugnard, president of Preferred Health Management, a preferred provider organization (PPO) consulting firm in Arlington, Virginia.

In 1987, VHA was celebrating its tenth anniversary, yet the managed care venture was sapping the group's financial strength. Not only was it requiring more and more capital, it was plunging the organization into debt. As acknowledged by Reed at the time, "The expectations for Partners were a lot higher than our ability to deliver."

Reed, a businessman steeped in self-assurance and Wall Street smarts, seemed to have it all figured out. VHAE could sell its stock at about 18 times earnings. The way he saw it, with just $1 of earnings, VHAE could sell $18 in equity. It then could borrow another $18 against the new equity, giving the company a comfortable 50 percent debt-to-capitalization ratio. Unfortunately, the nominal $1 in earnings was never realized.

One of the great ironies about VHA is that the strength of the investor-owned chains is what galvanized the group when it was founded in 1977. However, the desire to rip a page from the investor-owned playbook by tapping Wall Street with a public offering threatened the financial security of the alliance itself. What's more, the venture led to the ouster of Reed and the alliance's first full-time CEO, Don Arnwine. By the time Reed and

Arnwine were dismissed, VHAE had lost $87 million on revenues of $305 million.

VHA hired a California hospital system executive, Robert O'Leary, to turn the alliance around. He undid the tangled web of marginal ventures, either selling or closing down each of VHAE's several businesses. With the proceeds from the sale, he paid off VHA's debt of $17.6 million in late 1990 and early 1991. He also paid back the $1.8 million the hospitals had loaned to the alliance in 1983 and 1984 to cover cash flow. The remarkable turnaround of VHA got O'Leary a new job: president and CEO of AMI.

HUMANA PUSHES ON

VHA got out of the managed care business, as did HCA and AMI. However, Humana had made the biggest commitment to the insurance business, and company executives didn't want to admit they were wrong.

One of Humana Care Plus's biggest moves was in the Chicago market, where Humana put the infrastructure in place by buying a financially struggling chain of 29 urgent care centers (now they'd be called primary care clinics) called Doctors Officenters for $17 million. Humana changed the name to MedFirst Centers. These centers sprouted up in Chicago and other cities where Humana had its Care Plus insurance plan, treating plan enrollees in a less-expensive setting. In its 1985 annual report, Humana reported that the number of MedFirst Centers had grown from 68 to 148. Humana maintained that by the end of 1986, it would have 350.

Humana was on a roll, and so was Jones. In 1985, *Business Week* reported that Jones was one of the twenty-five highest paid executives in the country. He had made $18.1 million in salary and stock options in 1984. Even so, the business was starting to hemorrhage. In its fiscal year, 1985, the Louisville chain took a $24 million pretax charge on MedFirst and Care Plus development. In Humana's annual report, Jones professed:

"Staying the same is easy. Changing, getting better, requires vision, determination and sustained effort."

In its fiscal year, 1986, Humana reported its first year-to-year decline in profits ever: a 75 percent drop to $54 million. It was the company's silver anniversary, but there wasn't much to celebrate. In October, the once invincible chain announced it would take a pretax charge of $232 million for its fourth quarter ended September 30, 1986. The amount included after-tax charges of $70 million on Humana Care Plus, $40 million on the sale of 70 MedFirst Centers, and $21 million to write down the value of the chain's ill-fated hospital in Mexico City (another grand vision undermined by the plummeting value of the Mexican peso). In reality, 1986 was the worst year ever experienced by investor-owned hospitals. The big four (led by Humana's disastrous results) reported a $500 million drop in profits.

Ironically, one of the core reasons for starting Care Plus was to fill Humana hospitals, but that wasn't happening. In 1986, only 47 percent of Care Plus patients were admitted to a Humana hospital. Humana had planned on capturing 75 percent of the Care Plus business. In 1987, the 87-hospital chain continued to press on with its managed care strategy, buying a financially ailing Florida HMO, International Medical Centers, for $40 million.

That same year, *Business Week* declared that Jones had "seemed to lose his golden touch." The magazine also highlighted Jones in another way, noting that his pay was the highest, relative to a company's return to shareholders over the past three years. While Humana stock waned, Jones had taken in $17.7 million from 1984 through 1986. Most of it came through his exercise of stock options.

Meanwhile, HCA, NME, and AMI were all abandoning their half-hearted ventures into the managed care business. "It looks to me as if there isn't going to be any 'supermed,'" Thomas Frist Jr. told *The Wall Street Journal* in 1987. Perhaps the struggles of HCA and Humana were necessary growing pains for a relatively young industry. "Tommy Frist and David Jones defined the 1990s by their actions in the 1980s," said Volla. "They were just ahead of their time."

In retrospect, the Humana foray into the managed care/insurance business was significant for several reasons. First, even though the venture proved unprofitable in the early years, it would eventually prove more financially viable than the hospital business. As mentioned, the concept was sound, but the timing was premature.

Significantly, Humana's commitment to remain in the underwriting arena would eventually polarize the hospital segment and the insurance component, thus leading to the creation of a separate hospital division (known as Galen) and the eventual sale of the hospital segment of the business. Ironically, the move to diversify eventually led to divestiture of Humana's core business: hospitals.

Also relevant is the bitter taste that the Care Plus experience (of the 1980s) would leave for the future owners of Galen hospital, namely Columbia. As we will discuss in later chapters, the issue of owning the financing mechanism (i.e., the insurance function) is a controversial and divisive subject for the leaders of today's megafirms.

Humana's Care Plus proved to be not only a bellwether for the for-profit hospitals, but a precursor to a highly successful and wildly profitable segment of the industry, the risk-assuming component of healthcare financing. As fate (or fortune) would have it, where Humana was once chided for its apparent folly, hospitals and health systems now scurry to obtain the mechanism to accept risk and capitated contracts.

A RURAL RETURN ON INVESTMENT

When investor-owned chains buy hospitals in rural areas, the dynamics are completely different than those experienced in the city. Out in the country, a hospital may be the largest employer and the only source of medical care for miles. If it is an investor-owned hospital, it may also be the largest taxpayer in the community.

Not-for-profit hospital executives who berate investor-owned hospitals for not providing enough charity care don't have much to say in small-town America. An investor-owned hospital in that setting has little choice but to take all patients. On the other hand, if the company gets into trouble, the town is going to have trouble. A philosophy of "business knows best" may work in the oil business or the automobile business, but in healthcare, such a corporate attitude can be especially punitive for rural America. If the only hospital in town closes because of mismanagement or financial errors by the corporate chain, the town will suffer the consequences.

For the most part, the big hospital chains that grew in the 1970s and 1980s focused on the city, not the country. For example, in the mid-1980s, HMO guru Paul Ellwood proposed forming a National Rural Health System of America that would band together the purchasing clout of the nation's 2,700 rural hospitals. Some rural advocates maintained it was a good idea. Some were not as convinced. "Humana and HCA aren't going to be interested in the survival of rural hospitals," said Kevin Fickenscher, president-elect of the National Rural Health Association in the July 5, 1985, issue of *Modern Healthcare*. Obviously this didn't prove to be the case.

Investor-owned hospital chains did become interested in rural systems, but in the late 1980s that experience begot misfortune. Entrepreneurs tried to duplicate the success of the HCAs and AMIs on a smaller scale. The problem was, rural healthcare didn't pay as well as urban healthcare. The DRG system that proved financially beneficial to urban hospitals was disastrous for many rural facilities. In its initial configuration, Medicare had an urban bias when it came to DRG payments, even though rural hospitals depended more heavily on government reimbursement.

Some rural hospitals depended on Medicare for up to 80 percent of their revenues, yet they received 40 percent less than urban hospitals for the same services. Why such a discrepancy? Federal actuaries and Medicare reimbursement architects reasoned that rural hospital costs were 40 percent less than their urban counterparts. This, however, was not the case. Healthcare finance is complex, but it doesn't take an economics scholar to recognize the high percentage of fixed costs involved in a hospital's financial framework. What's more, rural hospital administrators couldn't play the averages in a 40-bed hospital that their colleagues did in a 400-bed hospital. One lingering patient running up $100,000 in bills could send a rural hospital's bottom line south in an instant.

In 1986, Texas led the nation with 18 hospital closures; 11 of them were rural facilities. The next year, another nine hospitals closed. Ironically, the closures spurred a search for saviors, which led to new enterprises such as Westworld Community Health Care, Gateway Medical, and National Healthcare. However, the relief provided by companies such as Lake Forest, California-based Westworld wasn't necessarily what these hospitals needed. Westworld typically bought the only hospital in a small town, then raised prices two or threefold.

Price-gouging allegations took on a life of their own. In South Dakota, the governor warned state employees about high charges at the state's three Westworld hospitals. One example he used was a $15.75 bill for one Tylenol capsule.

Insurers also balked at the stratospheric charges, but Westworld had priorities. Medicare wasn't covering its costs, and the company had 14 percent interest-rate junk bonds to pay off. Westworld also took Wall Street for an expensive spin around the block in 1986 when the company's stock fell from a high of $15.38 to 63 cents.

Of the three companies—Westworld, Gateway, and National—only the latter survived the 1980s. National, scarred by shareholder suits and saddled by heavy debt, had pulled all of the tricks in its day, though. At one point, *The Wall Street Journal* described how employees at one National hospital slipped into hospital beds when the company's New York bankers came for a tour so the hospital would seem busier and presumably more profitable. Apparently the resident administrator reasoned that if there were more patients (even if they were fabricated), the bankers would assume there was more revenue.

THE RISE AND FALL OF A RURAL CHAIN: NATIONAL HEALTHCARE

National's odyssey shows that the hospital industry is not exempt from expert salesmen who can, at least for a while, push all the right financial buttons. The salesman in this case was Stephen Phelps, who was the administrator of Southeast Alabama Medical Center (SAMC; a 400-bed hospital in Dothan, Alabama) before he started National. Dothan was an employee of Hospital Affiliates, which had a management contract to operate SAMC.

When Hospital Affiliates was bought by HCA in 1981, Phelps convinced the hospital's board to give the management contract to him. That action spawned National Healthcare, which swelled to 28 hospitals by the end of 1985 when it sold $40 million in junk bonds and went public—two financial windfalls shepherded through Wall Street by Drexel Burnham Lambert.

At the time, Phelps was just 35 years old. A year later (1986), *Inc.* magazine ranked National the nation's fifth fastest growing company. *Forbes* featured Phelps in its "Up & Comers" section under the headline "Wal-Mart hospitals." However, *Forbes* didn't coin that moniker. Phelps himself described his company as "the Wal-Mart of healthcare." The trouble was, Phelps was no Sam Walton—something that soon became clear to investors and his newly recruited president, Stanton Tuttle.

Tuttle had been a manager at Sears, Roebuck and Company before getting his master's degree in hospital administration at Duke University and racking up more than 15 years of impressive results at Humana, General Care Corporation, and eventually HCA. As president of HCA's psychiatric division, Tuttle was one of HCA's top three executives.

Phelps started calling Tuttle, urging him to come work for National. "I turned him down at least six different times," Tuttle, then president of HCA's psychiatric division, recalled. Eventually, the HCA executive gave in as Phelps assuaged any fears Tuttle had about the precarious business of small, rural hospitals. "He was as smooth a talker as ever existed . . . a super, super salesman," Tuttle said.

National's stock was hot on Wall Street. The venerable giants of the hospital industry—Humana, AMI, and HCA—were restructuring, and National looked like the next good bet for investors. Unfortunately, the underlying financial status revealed that the company was on very shaky financial footing. National's long-term debt was an incredible 191 percent of equity. Citicorp lent the company $150 million to buy hospitals; instead, National used the loan to pay bills.

When Tuttle joined the company in May 1986, he had no idea that the company's financial fortunes were only skin-deep. Between 1984 and 1986, National had purchased seventeen rural hospitals and four nursing homes at a total cost of $131 million, but none of these facilities made money. Added to this was the grim reality that National's hospitals were only one-third full, Medicare reimbursement was abysmal, and the company had overpaid HCA for underperforming facilities.

As a condition of his employment, Tuttle was able to recruit his own chief financial officer. He lured Robert Thornton Jr. away from Charter Medical Corporation, the Atlanta-based psychiatric hospital chain. For six months, Thornton and his auditors dove into National's books and reported the results directly to Tuttle. What they found wasn't good. The company had failed to take write-offs for bad debt and Medicare contractual allowances. (Contractual allowances are basically the difference between what hospitals bill Medicare and what they receive in reimbursement.)

Actually, National was losing money. In January 1987, Tuttle took his concerns in writing to the board, urging the company's directors to take the necessary write-offs in contractual allowances and bad debt. Rather than accept Tuttle's recommendations, however, the board listened to Phelps, who convinced the directors to have Thornton report directly to him (Phelps) and the board, rather than Tuttle. Eventually, on Sept. 3, 1987, National issued a press release saying that it would report a $19.5 million loss for the fourth quarter, which ended June 1987, citing write-offs for contractual allowances and loan costs as the major reasons for the shortfall.

In another one-paragraph press release the same day, National announced that Tuttle had resigned. The downhill slide accelerated as National faced a $635 million shareholder suit. Phelps resigned from the company, along with three of his vice presidents and two directors in October, 1987. At the time of Phelps's resignation, the company's stock was selling for less than 87 cents a share, just a shadow of its $17-per-share price in late 1986. Under new management, National eventually restructured its debt, selling about $80 million in bonds in 1992 to pay off its bankers.

HEALTHTRUST SWIMS AGAINST THE TIDE

Interestingly, HCA's spin-off, HealthTrust, managed to rise above the woes experienced by National, Gateway, and Westworld. Where these companies faltered, HealthTrust and its top executive, R. Clayton McWhorter, succeeded and subsequently defied the pundits. McWhorter was well acquainted with the rural hospital business, having begun his career as a hospital pharmacist in rural Georgia.

Former President Jimmy Carter, then a state legislator, was one of three members on a committee (in 1965) that hired McWhorter for his first job as a hospital administrator in Americus, Georgia (the same hospital where Carter's daughter, Amy, was born).

Five years later, Tommy Frist Jr., M.D., then executive vice president at HCA, recruited McWhorter to cross the line to investor-owned healthcare. After some hesitation, McWhorter agreed. Once in the HCA family, the former pharmacist rose quickly through the ranks.

By 1985, McWhorter was president and chief operating officer (COO) of HCA. About this time, HCA stock desperately needed a jolt, and HealthTrust was conceived as a way to provide it. HCA executives decided to keep their top 75 hospitals, and spin off the remaining 104 to the employees, in what would be the largest ESOP ever.

The ESOP financing for HealthTrust carried huge tax advantages, but that alone wouldn't float the company. It was up to HealthTrust's top managers—Clayton McWhorter, Charles Martin, and Don MacNaughton—to make these underperforming, primarily rural hospitals pay off.

Most of the company's debt carried interest rates of around 10 percent. To ensure that the company didn't sink under its own weight, Frist tossed in three "winners": Eastern Idaho Regional Medical Center, a new hospital (the only one) in Idaho Falls and the largest private facility outside Boise; Bayshore Medical Center in the Houston suburb of Pasadena, Texas; and Plantation General Hospital, a 264-bed facility just outside Fort Lauderdale. However, even these cash cows had some liabilities. For example, Plantation General was located in a highly competitive market that made its profitability status far from a sure thing.

Even though HealthTrust had more acute-care hospitals than HCA (which was now left with seventy-eight), HCA's had been far healthier. An analysis by SMG, a Chicago research firm, showed that HealthTrust hospitals only accounted for 39 percent of HCA's patient days. HealthTrust hospitals were smaller, with 133 beds on average, compared with 230 beds in the HCA hospitals. The HealthTrust facilities were also emptier: 46 percent full (average occupancy) compared with 59 percent full for HCA's remaining facilities.

The HealthTrust deal was announced in May, and immediately the triumvirate (McWhorter, Martin, and MacNaughton) started working. MacNaughton was the "gray hair" of the trio, being an experienced CEO whom McWhorter could learn from. "I had always been the operations guy," McWhorter said.

Charlie Martin, the newly formed company's COO, had been in development at HCA and needed to learn the operations of the new HealthTrust hospitals very quickly. Between May and September of 1985, every HealthTrust hospital administrator came to Nashville to meet with Martin for an hour or two. Martin soon became known for a quick financial mind, attention to details, and a low tolerance for those who didn't work for constant improvement. "No level of performance was such that it couldn't be improved," Martin said. "With the leverage we had, we didn't have the luxury of being on cruise control."

McWhorter and Martin took on a kind of good cop/bad cop team at HealthTrust. McWhorter was the kinder, gentler CEO who had formerly been the hospital administrators' leader as HCA's COO. Martin was more of a bulldog as the COO of the new company.

Within 18 months of HealthTrust's spin-off from HCA, 60 percent of the hospital CEOs had been replaced. "It's a good incentive," McWhorter acknowledged. Some hospital CEOs didn't even last until HealthTrust was actually formed in September. During the meetings with Martin in Nashville, a few were let go immediately. "A few basically said they weren't interested in working any harder," Martin said.

In the ensuing months, Martin's scrutiny of the hospital CEOs didn't let up. He maintained that "a lot of them didn't seem accustomed to going through month by month, department by department, looking at where the money went." Because most of the HealthTrust hospitals operated in rural communities, Martin could make comparisons, especially for hospitals that were in the same size town or had a similar patient case mix.

Notwithstanding the high turnover, HealthTrust used a carrot as well as a stick for its hospital CEOs. The company increased the incentive compensation, allowing them to earn up to 80 percent of their salary in bonuses.

Meanwhile, McWhorter and others worked on paring away the weakest links. In the next three and a half years, HealthTrust sold twenty hospitals. Interestingly, two of them were in El Paso. They were the first two hospitals purchased by Rick Scott and his fledgling Columbia Hospital Corporation in July 1988. (Making a silk purse out of a sow's ear, Scott turned El Paso into the cornerstone of his company that eventually logged $20 billion in annual revenues.)

In any case, HealthTrust did better without the El Paso facilities. Rural hospitals continued to struggle, and 41 of them closed in 1988. Yet HealthTrust's prospects improved, and in December 1991 the company went public again, raising more than $500 million. HealthTrust methodically paid down its $2 billion debt burden. By the end of August 1992, the company's debt-to-equity ratio was 67 percent, down from 95 percent immediately following the spin-off from HCA.

In early 1994, HealthTrust joined the merger sweeps and offered to buy Epic Healthcare Group. Epic had spun off of AMI in September 1988 and never made money. Like HealthTrust, it was financed through an ESOP, which gave the firm significant tax breaks. One significant difference between the two companies was that while HealthTrust's Martin kept hospital administrators on a short operational leash, Epic corporate executives gave them free rein.

EPIC HEALTHCARE'S STRUGGLES

To look at Epic and HealthTrust was a study in contrasts. Relations between HCA's Frist and HealthTrust's McWhorter remained friendly from day one of the spin-off. HealthTrust shared information services and group purchasing with its former parent, which owned 10.7 million shares in the spin-off until 1992.

HCA had seemed like family for some of its executives. For example, when HealthTrust shares were languishing in the stock market, McWhorter turned to Frist for advice. Frist recommended Marilyn Herbert, who McWhorter promptly hired as his investor relations director. Nevertheless, there was a degree of antagonism on the part of HealthTrust executives toward the former parent, HCA, which had set them adrift (in a seemingly ill-equipped craft). Acknowledged McWhorter: "We were just hell-bent that we were going to get up early every morning and beat HCA. If HCA's supply costs per day were a certain amount, we were going to beat it."

Although HealthTrust managers may have manifested some ill will toward HCA, it was nothing like the divisiveness that festered between Epic and AMI. When AMI decided to spin off Epic, company officials summoned all the hospital executive directors to Dallas. In a hotel outside the Dallas/Fort Worth International Airport, AMI officials called out the names of thirty-seven executive directors. They were told to go into another room with Kenn George. That's how they found out they were leaving AMI.

George, who headed AMI's southwestern division, was given the top spot to lead the spin-off of Epic. The relationship between Epic and AMI continued to deteriorate. Perhaps AMI's revolving door of executives made any relationship impossible; perhaps Epic wanted to stand on its own. Even after AMI moved its headquarters to Dallas, executives from the two companies didn't visit each other's offices. AMI had a senior executive, Alan Chamison, on Epic's board, but he was mainly keeping tabs on AMI's investment. At one point AMI, which retained a 26 percent stake in Epic, sued company officials over their compensation plan. AMI later dropped the suit, declining to discuss the circumstances surrounding the action.

Under the direction of Kenn George, a West Texan who walked in cowboy boots and sometimes rode a motorcycle to work, Epic hung on, generating cash, but doing little to wipe off its massive debt load. The company was regarded by some as a bunch of cowboys, a sentiment accentuated by the collection of western paintings and sculptures located in the Dallas headquarters. When HealthTrust bought Epic in May 1994, it wasn't surprising that HealthTrust executives gave Epic executives rodeo belt buckles as going-away presents. George himself had been a former rodeo rider who gravitated to the oil business in Midland, Texas, before joining AMI. He moved from cutting horses to polo ponies but stayed active in the state's Republican Party and was known to harbor political ambitions.

HealthTrust required hospital CEOs to have a management plan and a strategic plan. The CEOs were held accountable for their hospital's financial performance. In contrast, many of the financial functions (such as accounts payable) for Epic hospitals were handled out of the Dallas office. That meant the EDs at Epic didn't worry about them as much as their counterparts at HealthTrust.

HealthTrust held seminars on the quality of a hospital's balance sheet. Anyone tampering with their numbers was automatically terminated. Conversely, George's freewheeling style filtered through the corporate culture of Epic, which stressed employee ownership much more than HealthTrust. Although Epic's hospital administrators had budgets, insiders said there were few consequences for those who didn't meet them. One executive quipped that the best incentive was to let a hospital know it was up for sale. Telling the managers at hospitals in Alice, Texas, and Hope, Arkansas, that they were on the sale block produced an "incredible turnaround," he said.

Epic officials also would claim that their hospitals were in worse shape than HealthTrust's. While HealthTrust was stacked with the three previously mentioned, large moneymakers, only one of Epic's hospitals had more than 150 beds, and that one was not exactly a jewel, as it was slated for sale from the very beginning.

Despite its huge debt burden, Epic had favorable cash flow within the first six months of the separation from AMI. During that time, George and his top executives were piling up stock appreciation rights (SARs) that would build in value despite the company's weak financial condition. Unlike stock options that don't kick in unless the stock reaches a set price, SARs were awarded free to company executives with no such requirements.

Merger fever hit the hospital chains in 1993, and Epic was regarded by several suitors. However, the company's debt (some of it financed at sky-high 15 percent interest rates) held many of the would-be buyers at bay. Even so, the rumor mill got so hot that at one point in November 1993 George issued a memo to employees: "Investment bankers are rotating through my office like hamsters on a treadmill. Every one of them is hot on a deal and sniffing for a big fee. The perfect deal is just ahead of us! Yeah! Heck, my mother and father even called with an idea. Gads, people! Go back to work."

Merger mania filled the air. HealthTrust's McWhorter had been weighing a bid for governor of Tennessee. When his board insisted he decide between the gubernatorial race and running HealthTrust, he chose HealthTrust. HealthTrust was getting offers, but McWhorter decided to turn the tables. "I needed to take the initiative," he said.

McWhorter and his board offered to buy Epic in January 1994 for approximately $1 billion. For Epic, it was like manna from heaven, as well as a godsend for AMI and especially George, who walked away with $23 million in cash the day of the transaction, largely because of his SARs. AMI cashed in $43 million for its stake.

The deal bulked up HealthTrust's size by a third, putting it in the big leagues of hospital companies. Once the merger was completed in May of 1994, HealthTrust executives cleaned house at Epic. A condition of the deal was that Epic's top twelve executives would be terminated. Once HealthTrust was in charge, one-third of the hospital CEOs were also replaced. "Bottom line, the company was not very well managed," McWhorter said. "They took their eye off the core business."

HealthTrust's success proved that rural hospitals could be managed successfully by investor-owned chains. Importantly, by the early 1990s, the financial wind was at the backs of rural hospitals. Trying to compensate for past wrongs, Congress put a payment scheme into motion that increased Medicare reimbursement to rural hospitals. That modification, along with a complicated but financially beneficial geographic reclassification edict, helped rural hospitals become profitable again. In 1992 rural hospitals had a higher profit margin than their urban counterparts.

Interestingly, National Healthcare restructured and changed its name to Hallmark Healthcare. Subsequently, in 1994, the newly named company sold out to another investor-owned chain, Community Health Systems, that focused on rural and suburban areas. By the mid-1990s, Community Health Systems and Health Management Associates had demonstrated success in rural markets, and much of the taint left on small towns by investor-owned firms such as Westworld had faded. (Health Management Associates is addressed in a later chapter.)

"Most hospital boards today couldn't tell you who Westworld or Gateway was," says Steve Taylor, president of Brim, the Portland-based firm that specializes in managing rural hospitals. That short-term memory, coupled with an attitude change, has made rural hospitals fertile ground once again for investor-owned chains in the late 1990s. "Rural communities used to have the attitude that the hospital was akin to the local high school," Taylor noted. "You wouldn't think about selling the high school," he said, adding, "Now, they view the hospital as a complicated business. Sure, it has social welfare values, but they're (community residents) thinking about it differently."

The main reason this review of investor-owned rural hospital history is highly relevant is that rural hospitals in the late 1990s may feel insulated from the need to form strategic alliances. Executives at these facilities may not think that Columbia or any other system is interested in their facility because of geographic setting or size. In truth, the merger between HealthTrust and Columbia/HCA sounded a clarion call to small and rural hospitals throughout the country that everyone is now fair game.

As noted, HealthTrust has proven that rural and small hospitals can make a profit. On top of that, with purchaser coalitions being formed in large areas as well as small, the need for extensive geographic diversity is high and increasing. Consequently, smaller hospitals in the United States (even those located in rural locations) will round out the network for many regional systems. Fundamentally, rural hospitals need to assess the strategic advantage of alliances and linkages as much as their urban counterparts, if not more so. If the administrators at rural facilities fail to thoroughly evaluate the benefits of increased market leverage available through network involvement, they may find their facility locked out of crucial managed care contracts.

As pointed out earlier, a fair number of smaller facilities have faced the unfortunate proposition of having to close their doors because they could not compete on cost or breadth of services. Given the increased emphasis on cost containment, that trend will no doubt continue. Hospitals and health systems that will likely weather the storms of reform (market-led reform) will be those that expand their geographic and operational bases, broaden their financial networks, and achieve significant economies of scale. In summary, it is predicted that the stand-alone hospital will not stand alone long. It will either choose to affiliate or eventually disintegrate.

2
CHAPTER

Columbia Agitates and Motivates the Industry

Move over Hillary . . . Rick Scott is about to reform American healthcare.

Russell Coile Jr., healthcare futurist, 1995

As any entrepreneur knows, change breeds opportunity. This is especially applicable in the healthcare field, where entrepreneurs, both honorable and not so honorable, lurk at every turn. Among the would-be "Waltons" of healthcare are doctors, nurses, pharmacists, therapists, billing clerks, and ambulance drivers. If pressed, each can tip an alert investor to some way to turn a buck in this business.

Teeming with cash flow and mismanagement, healthcare is an entrepreneur's paradise. Within a trillion-dollar industry, there's always a better, cheaper way to do something. All you need is the right code so you can bill for it, or so some would argue.

Amid these throngs of entrepreneurs came Richard Scott, who founded Columbia Hospital Corporation in 1987. When Scott entered healthcare, hospital companies were out of favor. Doom and gloom filled the air as hospital profits plummeted both in the not-for-profit and investor-owned sectors. Shareholders who had invested in the large hospital chains were grumbling, and their executives were sweating over restructuring plans.

Scott's goal was to change the entire healthcare industry, which in retrospect, sounds a bit pretentious. However, Scott was determined—maybe too determined. Starting with 6 A.M. meetings, he drove himself and others hard. He visited at least 100 hospitals a year, sent out hundreds of e-mails a week, and met with employees, physicians, and patients constantly.

"Everything we're doing is changing the status quo," Scott told a group of investment bankers and money managers in late 1996. That created enemies because "a lot of people are doing real well with the status quo." At the Bear Stearns Health Care Conference, Scott gave his synopsis of the company's strategy: Be daring, be first, be different.

Arguably, no one upset the industry more than Rick Scott. Some paid homage to him as a business genius who forced the industry to shape up. At this particular conference, Columbia was the reigning champ. Its board had just approved a three-for-two stock split, and the industry was in a massive consolidation with Columbia in the lead. Columbia had recently launched its branding campaign and provided a toll-free phone number (1-800-Columbia), designed to make consumers aware of this rising giant. Columbia was becoming consumer oriented, a concept that was foreign to many hospital systems.

Scott was the luncheon speaker on this day, zigzagging his way through the crowded room of 1,000 people. At his table of 10, the awe with which he was regarded was obvious. Whenever he spoke, everyone at the table stopped talking and leaned to hear what he had to say. Wall Street was adoring.

On Main Street U.S.A., however, the detractors were getting more ardent, and state officials were starting to step in Columbia's way. Even so, Scott seemed up to the challenge. From the beginning, he had taken on the $400 billion hospital industry, which was overwhelmingly dominated by not-for-profit organizations. He knew it would be an uphill battle from the start.

THE COLUMBIA STORY

It's a cold, grey February morning in Louisville, Kentucky, and Columbia Healthcare Corporation is just days away from finalizing its merger with one of the legends of the investor-owned healthcare industry: Hospital Corporation of America (HCA). Columbia's founder, Richard Scott, casually steps from a snow-pocketed parking lot and into the brightly lit lobby of Audubon Regional Medical Center. The building looks like just another suburban hospital in Columbia's growing chain, but it isn't.

This is where Humana made history nearly 10 years earlier (December 1984), when the world lingered on every heartbeat of William Schroeder, the world's second artificial heart transplant recipient. At that time, Humana founders David Jones and Wendell Cherry reveled in the media bonfire that spread across hundreds of newspapers and magazines. The contrast between the Humana founders and Scott couldn't be more stark. Growing up in Kansas City, Missouri, Scott used to sit in the back of the classroom so he wouldn't be noticed. He's a proud man, but unpretentious—definitely not Humana-like, even though he's taken over all of its hospitals.

On this day in February, Scott seems to feel especially awkward. A video crew is following him around as he roves the hospital, shaking hands with clerks in the admissions department and food handlers in the cafeteria. As he's being taped for an employee video about health reform, Scott smiles often, but never at the camera. He's seen talking to his employees in a friendly but not overbearing manner even though he's obviously the boss here. Who would think this man was recently named one of the "most feared" in the city by *Louisville Magazine*? (Humana founder Jones was voted the "most feared.")

As Scott chats with employees, he hands out a few lapel pins. The one-inch pins consist of the word *Columbia* in gold, underlined with a red stripe. Scott picked the name himself when starting the company in 1987. It was a name that sounded formidable, and in seven short years, it had grown to meet that description.

Like Scott, the pins are understated, like those diminutive *McDonald's* signs seen in suburbs where zoning laws forbid restaurants to erect the giant yellow arches. Eventually, the HCA letters will be added to the Columbia pins, making them slightly longer, but little else. The effect is similar with the company: larger with HCA, but basically unchanged. Even in the combined behemoth that became Columbia/HCA, Scott, his crew, and his strategy remained in control.

When a woman in the cafeteria asks for a pin, Scott discovers he's all out. Without hesitation, he reaches up to his own, unfastens it, and offers it to her. She's clearly delighted. Not everyone is delighted, however, with Columbia's ascent and accompanying clout. The hospital industry still consists of 85 percent tax-exempt hospitals, and the rumblings about Columbia and its mounting clout grow stronger with each passing month. Not-for-profit hospitals don't like his growth, his confidence, or his questions regarding whether their organizations "live up" to their tax exemptions.

Down deep, Scott's detractors believe Columbia will falter. These investor-owned giants always seem to falter: HCA, Humana, National Medical Enterprises (NME), and American Medical International (AMI). They stumbled when they became greedy, or upset Wall Street, or just got tired of the core business and strayed into unproven territory.

Still, even some of the skeptics used to wonder, "When will that happen to Columbia? And what if Scott doesn't stumble? What if he just keeps buying and buying?" Up through 1995, Scott's Columbia had consumed Galen, HCA, and HealthTrust. It was the 800-pound (and $20 billion) gorilla in a $400 billion hospital industry.

"I look at this as a marathon, and we're very early in it," said the 42-year-old lawyer turned health market magnate in 1995. Now equal in size to health industry giants like Johnson & Johnson and Merck, Columbia was becoming as much a part of consumers' lives as some fast-food restaurant chains.

Initially, Columbia's footprints were not nearly as obvious, though. The company was more of a stealth corporation. It owned 300-plus hospitals, yet only industry insiders could go from town to town identifying which were Columbia facilities and which were not. That changed, of course, with the branding campaign of 1996.

After its acquisition of HealthTrust in 1995, Columbia/ HCA Healthcare Corporation was already the nation's 10th largest employer, a $16 billion company. By 1997, it was the seventh largest with $20 billion in revenues, and word was that the $100 billion milestone was in Scott's business plan.

It's interesting to note how far this industry has come. When Medicare was approved in 1965, all of the hospitals in America together generated revenues of $13 billion. Now Columbia/HCA, one company with less than seven percent of the nation's hospitals, generates annual revenues that eclipse that amount.

By 1994, Scott had built a company nearly everyone in the industry was talking about. In an October 30, 1994, profile in *The New York Times,* Scott was hailed as "the de facto czar of cost containment" and the "unelected champion of the relentlessly free market." The article itself carried the headline: "Now, It's the Rick Scott Health Plan." That type of press definitely chafed not-for-profit executives who believed Scott was usurping the credit they deserved for marketplace health reform. In some not-for-profit board rooms, Scott became public enemy number one.

"Up until now, they've just been eating their young," scoffed Mack Haning, a senior director at VHA, the nation's largest alliance of not-for-profit hospitals with 1,000 members. In a VHA publication, the organization called Scott a "zealot." They downplayed his influence, saying that not-for-profit hospitals have been doing for years what Scott was grandstanding about: consolidation, networking, and cost control.

Arguably, much of what they said was true. Rick Scott did not introduce consolidation to the hospital industry, nor did he invent the concept of networking among providers. However, he did introduce one element that changed everything in the mid-1990s: speed. Like the runaway bus in the 1994 hit movie *Speed,* Columbia/HCA gave competitors little choice. They had to consolidate or get out of the way. "It appears that I'm changing the industry," Scott said at one point, adding, "All I'm doing is responding to changes in the industry."

Take New Orleans, for example, where three of the city's largest not-for-profit hospitals decided to merge in 1995. They agreed that managed care would probably have forced providers to eventually combine their operations. However, they looked around and saw Columbia cutting a deal with Tulane University Medical Center and NME negotiating with Louisiana State University's medical center. Peter Betts, president and CEO of one of the three merger partners, East Jefferson General Hospital, commented, "We realized our time frame was a lot shorter because everybody was choosing up sides. We weren't sure there would be partners left to choose from."

SCOTT'S PERSONA EMBODIES COLUMBIA

On the heels of the 1980s era, when hospital managers acted more like colleagues than competitors, Scott's Columbia emerged. In the wake of failed ventures into the insurance business and hospital chains that survived because they just kept raising charges higher and higher, Columbia flourished. Before Columbia moved to Nashville in 1995, Scott's office in Louisville overlooked the placid Ohio River, the same river Jones and Cherry likely pondered when building Humana in its halcyon days. The similarities seem to end there.

Humana's corporate headquarters looms over downtown Louisville. When Humana split in 1993, the insurance company stayed in the plush corporate offices, and the hospital company, called Galen Healthcare, moved to more modest digs down the street. Humana's stylish $50-million office building, which some locals have dubbed the "Pink Privy," seems an anachronism in the 1990s and certainly contrary to Scott's style.

Humana's headquarters weren't an anomaly among for-profit chains, however. In Beverly Hills, California, AMI's corporate offices at one time were just off the elite Rodeo Drive and featured such executive perks as an in-house chef. "I don't like to spend money," Scott retorted when asked about his plain-vanilla corporate offices. Then he added, "I don't think I'm going to change."

Kansas physician Raymond Lumb recalls visiting Scott's office while considering a deal in November 1994 between his 74-physician group practice (the second largest in the state) and Columbia. Initially, he and his partners had their doubts. "Columbia is so big. There's a lot of fear, a lot of misinformation," Lumb said. Then, they went to Louisville. "He [Scott] had plastic laminated lamps and a metal file cabinet," said Lumb. Somehow, you get the feeling that Lumb had been in the offices of plenty of not-for-profit CEOs whose penny-pinching wasn't as evident.

In an industry that nearly everyone acknowledges wastes millions of dollars every year, Scott donned the image of a coupon clipper. In a *Fortune* article in which Columbia was ranked as the fourteenth fastest growing company in 1994, Scott's penny-pinching came out when he revealed that he saves the paper clips from his mail. Wall Street took notice of the potential of what Scott could wring from a trillion-dollar industry. Savings equal profits; profits render higher stock prices.

"We're going to be a very volume-oriented company," Scott told stock analysts in early 1994. Increasing volume means lower costs, he said, adding, "We want to get ourselves into a position where everyone wants to do business with us." By demanding discounts from everyone—cardiac equipment suppliers to head hunters—Scott believed his hospitals could lower the cost of doing business. Such a strategy will put Columbia "in a position that no one has ever been in in this industry," he said flatly.

Lindy Richardson, the company's senior vice president of public affairs, said that when she had a problem, she told Scott she wanted to talk to some people to get some ideas. "OK," Scott replied, "Talk to some people in your department." In other words, don't waste money on outside consultants.

Vendors sometimes complained that Columbia executives were heavy-handed. The attitude was, in essence, "We're Columbia. You can deal with us on our terms or not deal with us. And, by the way, we want a discount." "Part of our success has been that we've been very cost-conscious," Scott explained. "We do expect a discount." Scott's call to cut costs—not a little but a lot, as he said in his 1994 TV commercials—couldn't have been more timely. Columbia/HCA's rise coincided with a period of unusually low healthcare inflation. In 1993 and 1994, the medical care component of the Consumer Price Index rose just five percent, the smallest increase in 20 years. Scott kept tabs on that index, sending memos to hospital CEOs, reminding them that there was little room to raise charges or costs.

THE FIRST BID FOR HCA

Richard Scott acquired some of his nuts-and-bolts business sense working in a doughnut shop in college. There's not much room for wasteful spending when you're charging a buck or two for a dozen glazed.

After graduating from Southern Methodist University law school, Scott joined Dallas's largest law firm in 1977, Johnson & Gibbs, and began cutting his teeth on healthcare securities, acquisitions, and financial arrangements. After 10 years, he wearied of being on the sidelines, so Scott and two former Republic Health Corporation executives, Richard Ragsdale and Charles Miller, offered $3.9 billion ($47 a share) for HCA.

Scott had lined up financing with Citicorp and Drexel Burnham Lambert, which at the time was known as Wall Street's junk bond rainmaker. Even though HCA's board appeared not to take the bid seriously, Scott later maintained, "We were comfortable that all the money was there." Even so, HCA turned the trio down cold. In reflection, "It's funny how these things come around a different way," said Charles Kane, who had been an HCA board member at the time and later served on the Columbia board. Ironically, Scott eventually ran the company that includes HCA. However, at that time, HCA's president and CEO Thomas Frist Jr., M.D., had no intention of letting HCA fall into other hands.

The trio cordially exited, describing the HCA bid as no more than a "friendly overture." Of that ambitious trio, Scott was the unknown in the industry. Both Ragsdale and Miller were known in the small world of hospital corporations.

Despite his anonymity, Scott had worthy credentials from Ragsdale, Republic's cofounder. Ragsdale later went on to found another hospital chain, Community Health Systems, out of Houston, Texas. Ragsdale knew how Scott, who had been Republic's outside counsel, worked through the night to get Republic's $45 million initial public offering done in 1983. Republic wanted to sell its stock on July 1 before a long Fourth of July weekend. The timing proved fortuitous. Republic stock opened at $23 a share, and never traded higher. The push ensured that Republic raised the most cash.

After the failed HCA bid, Scott moved on. Miller, however, soon got a call from Fort Worth financial whiz Richard Rainwater. "At first, it didn't hit me who he was," Miller recalls. Then he remembered seeing the former chief adviser to the Bass brothers on the cover of one of the national business magazines. Rainwater, with an MBA from Stanford, had helped the oil-rich Bass family build its $5 billion empire by dealing in huge chunks of Disney and Texaco stock. He left to start his own investment company in 1986.

"I was referred to you by Tommy Frist," Rainwater told Miller, and then explained why he had called. Rainwater wanted to start a hospital company, and the idea sounded just intriguing enough to Miller. He accepted Rainwater's invitation to discuss the idea at a getaway in Nantucket, Massachusetts, at an old beach motel that Rainwater owned.

"Look, I know Republic had its problems," Rainwater declared. Then he commended Miller on knowing "when to get out," referring to Miller's departure before Republic's ill-fated leveraged buyout (LBO) in late 1986. Rainwater added that he sensed Miller was "smart enough to get off the track before the train wreck." With much to think about, Miller returned to Houston. Finally, he called Rainwater back and turned him down. "I just don't have the appetite to do it again," Miller told him. Rainwater wasn't ready to give up, though. "Can you recommend somebody I can talk to?" he asked. To which Miller responded, "There is a guy I know who is young, smart, sharp, aggressive. His name is Rick Scott."

A FORMIDABLE PARTNERSHIP: SCOTT AND RAINWATER

Rainwater drove to Dallas to visit the potential partner. "The offer was to share an office with him," Scott recalled. The two men would start a hospital company together; no commitment was made about financing. Scott didn't hesitate and accepted the offer in one day. Somewhat inauspiciously, the Rainwater/Scott partnership began on October 19, 1987, on Black Monday—the day the Dow Jones average fell 500 points.

The time wasn't all that great for hospitals either. In 1987, only half of the nation's hospitals made a profit on patient operations. Many were struggling with Medicare's new prospective payment system, which paid them a set price based on a patient's diagnosis. The cost-plus days of charging Medicare were already over. Medicare margins had been in the 14 percent range in 1984. By 1987, they had dropped to 5 percent, according to federal figures.

The industry was in a slump, but Rainwater believed the culprit was management, or rather, mismanagement. Both he and Scott saw an opportunity to make a run at the struggling industry, which is exactly what they did. In addition to starting Columbia, Rainwater became an equity investor in AMI, and in 1989 he put up $28 million to help Frist and his managers take HCA private in a $4 billion deal.

Nashville banker and former HCA board member Kane remembers having lunch with Rainwater after they had both attended an HCA board meeting and shortly after Rainwater started Columbia with Scott. "He [Rainwater] was talking about the concept and what they were going to do," stated Kane, and added, "They felt in the changing healthcare world you needed to be innovative. The concept was good."

Columbia became Rainwater's most profitable deal. By mid-1994, Columbia was Rainwater's biggest personal holding, according to *Business Week*. Of a nearly $800 million portfolio, his Columbia investment represented $320 million. Miller later laughed about it, saying the biggest mistake he ever made was introducing Scott to Rainwater. Ironically, Miller did get back into the hospital business. He now heads Paracelsus Healthcare Corporation, a Houston-based firm, which is described in Chapter 6.

It was the 30-something Scott, however, who took the initiative in 1987, working from Rainwater's 20th-floor offices on Main Street in Fort Worth. The building was one of two towers sheathed in blue-tinted glass and built by the multibillionaire Bass brothers.

Rainwater's company, Investment Limited Partnership, was full of young Turks, some of whom became millionaires through their ability to buy and sell securities. Regarded as the "Baghdad Bazaar," Rainwater's trading room was full of these men, with their eyes fixed on computer screens, buying and selling stocks, bonds, and even companies. From his office on the 20th floor, Scott did his own buying of hospitals.

Perhaps no one in the history of healthcare has ever tried so relentlessly to enter the hospital business as Scott. In November 1987, Scott wrote 1,000 letters to people he thought might be interested in selling him their hospitals. He received no favorable responses. "I tried everything. I called everybody. I flew all over the place," Scott recounted with frustration evident in his voice. Retelling the experience several years later, Scott hadn't forgotten how arduous the effort was, especially for a man as impatient as he is.

Married with two school-age children, Scott knew it all hinged on him to get the business underway. He went to hospital meetings, dinners, and lunches, hoping to connect with the right people who would open the door to an opportunity . . . even a crack.

EARLY WINS IN EL PASO

Finally, Scott's tenacity paid off. A group of physicians in El Paso wanted to build a new hospital, but Scott talked them out of it. "I told them the more logical thing is we ought to go and try to buy an existing hospital," Scott said. *Logical* and *rational* were

Scott's buzz words, and he used them at nearly every turn. Scott then called R. Clayton McWhorter, top executive at HealthTrust, which just prior to Columbia's creation was formed to take the underperforming castoffs of HCA. HealthTrust was now discarding the hospitals it didn't want, so in essence, Scott purchased what some considered the dregs of the industry barrel—two HealthTrust hospitals in El Paso.

To finance the deal, Scott and Rainwater each put up $125,000 and formed a partnership with a group of 110 physicians in El Paso. The partnership bought the two hospitals from HealthTrust, financed with $65 million from Citicorp in July 1988. El Paso was the maiden voyage and became the prototype for the soon-to-be corporate giant. For Columbia, it was akin to the McDonald's hamburger or the Federal Express overnight letter.

Scott rarely talked about Columbia without mentioning the city where it all began. "What we're going to do is continue to focus like we did in El Paso," Scott often repeated. The El Paso arrangement laid three cornerstones that were the building blocks for Scott's $20 billion company: physician ownership, consolidation, and local market management.

Of the three, physician ownership would be the most controversial. Critics excoriated Scott for trying to buy patient referrals through physician partnerships. Yet, he calmly explained that doctors order medical care, demand expensive equipment, and significantly influence healthcare costs. Making them financial partners would get doctors to think twice before demanding another multimillion-dollar laser or radiology suite. The participating physicians' return (from the partnership) depended on the amount of their investment, not the amount of patient referrals, he added.

By and large, doctors are an entrepreneurial breed. They want independence, and they want to be rewarded for their initiative. Arguably, Scott merely tapped into that desire, which some simply dismissed as greed. However, he also tapped into their desire to be part of the decision-making process at hospitals. Some hospital administrators had grown up in the business viewing physicians as adversaries. Scott's approach was, "Let's be on the same team."

All that notwithstanding, a partnership with physicians can be a no-win situation. Often, providers have found that if they refuse to enter into business deals with their doctors, the doctors will simply find another provider that's willing (the any-willing-partner approach). On the other hand, if hospitals do enter a business deal with their physicians, other providers may accuse them of attempting to buy referrals. It's a fine line to walk, yet hospitals that want to survive must find a way to develop a partnership with their medical staff.

Historically, hospitals and physicians have had a somewhat unique relationship. Hospitals are the only business in which people who are not employees (the doctors) can come in and give orders to the employees (nurses, technicians, etc.) and consume their supplies. Oddly enough, administrators and physicians are sometimes at odds with each other in an eternal power struggle. It was kind of an "I need you more than you need me" attitude for both parties. The dynamics of the present-day market have, however, necessitated that hospitals and physicians act in concert (in what is termed "vertical integration") to present a continuum of care and an integrated system that can be offered to managed care companies.

In response to the changing needs of the market, and to counter some of the historical divergence between doctors and hospitals, the large chains, including Epic, HealthTrust, and Republic, initiated physician joint ventures, although none did so with the fervor of Columbia. AMI and NME also tried doctor partnerships but never matched Columbia's success.

In reality, some physician joint ventures were little more than window dressing. Physicians received a financial stake but not a true say in business. Scott aimed to make his physician arrangements more of a partnership, not just financially but operationally; although that's not to underestimate the financial ties. "Physicians are going to be motivated to find alternatives that meet their long-term security needs," noted Denny Shelton, Columbia/HCA's central group president. As physicians' incomes are pressed by managed care payors, they were likely to look for other financially satisfying avenues. Columbia was a boulevard for those.

In Florida's Broward County, Columbia had hoped to raise $16 million in 1994 by selling a 20 percent stake in its network of five hospitals, a home healthcare agency, and a surgery center. To Columbia's surprise, 450 physicians wanted in and were willing to invest $30 million, an amount that would have represented a substantial equity offering on Wall Street. In a sense, Columbia's first partnership in El Paso established the precedent for physician partnerships.

CONSOLIDATION: A CORE CEMENT IN COLUMBIA'S STRATEGY

Another hallmark of Columbia's market strategy occurred in El Paso. After only five months, Columbia bought Landmark Medical Center (a financially weakened hospital that was in danger of losing its Medicare accreditation) for $11 million. The struggling hospital had 355 beds and only 54 patients. Scott promptly closed Landmark and moved the patients over to his other two hospitals. Thus was born another Columbia cornerstone: consolidation.

In El Paso, Scott bought three hospitals and shut one down. Later, in Miami, Columbia merged the operations of Victoria Hospital and Cedars Medical Center— a strategy that might be alien to most hospital companies, where closing hospitals was considered negative. Yet, Scott proved how consolidation boosted cash flow by $3 million in Miami as inpatient and outpatient services were reallocated. If the government had forced hospitals to merge and close beds, hospital leaders and statesmen alike would have been indignant, screaming about the ominous connotations. Yet in 1994, market-driven consolidation, pushed by Columbia, occurred in city after city.

Investor-owned hospitals such as Columbia's weren't the only ones merging. Worried about Columbia, not-for-profit hospitals began looking around for merger partners. Sometimes the parties were motivated by financial considerations—if their census was dropping or HMOs were cutting their payments. However, more often than not, hospital executives and board members were worried about Columbia. Columbia was the straw that stirred the drink. "We're going to liven things up 100 percent of the time when we're in the marketplace," promised Scott's right-hand man, COO David Vandewater.

Another strategy that separated Columbia was its approach to networks or systems in individual markets. In the past, investor-owned chains had been somewhat like corporate vagabonds. They bought one hospital here, one there. Their facilities were spread all over the map. Obviously, for these early systems the priority was not buying hospitals and consolidating them; it was collecting them, building volume, and making profits. Columbia took a different approach.

Columbia's determination to concentrate on single markets and consolidate hospitals proved a bit risky, though, because a side effect was limiting competition. That ensuing consequence predictably raised the specter of antitrust scrutiny from the federal government—something with which Columbia would become very familiar as the company developed.

This third cornerstone, local market development and management, worked hand in glove with consolidation. Scott didn't stop with hospitals and physicians in El Paso. He soon opened an 80-bed psychiatric hospital, acquired two outpatient diagnostic centers, and began construction on a three-story cancer center. All of this activity was under the control of a local market manager. "The key is [to] give decision-making power to local management teams. Act like a small company," Scott maintained.

In El Paso, the manager was Russell Schneider, a former Methodist Hospital executive with seemingly boundless energy. Schneider prospered under the authority and autonomy handed to him by Scott. Each Columbia market would soon have its own market manager. In Dallas, Scott installed former Humana regional executive Gary Hill; in Houston, another former Methodist executive, Jay Grinney; in Louisville, former

Erlanger Medical Center CEO, James Pickle. Each region had its own president, COO, and chief financial officer (CFO). This represented a different approach from the way most investor-owned companies had operated. In traditional for-profit systems, regional vice presidents typically had authority over hospital administrators in their area, yet there was little attempt to work as a team.

Interestingly, Scott structured Columbia/HCA in the way HCA had wanted to restructure itself in the late 1980s. In his book *Management Dimensions,* co-author and then chairman of Healthtrust, Clayton McWhorter, discussed the corporate structure of HCA. The company was divided into four sections: the HCA Psychiatric Corporation, two divisions of owned hospitals, and a division of managed hospitals. HCA had been considering restructuring into one division in which there were four regions, each with its own president; an international division with its own president; and a product specialization division with its own president.

The latter corporate structure is how Columbia/HCA was organized under Scott. McWhorter argued in his book that such a structure would be more responsive to local needs, keeping executives more motivated and enhancing the company's corporate image by keeping operations closer to the markets served. HCA didn't convert to that outlined structure because the resulting upheaval would have been too extensive, McWhorter wrote.

Investor-owned chains too often have operated with layers of mid-level managers, senior managers, and executive managers. In many cases, this bureaucracy left hospital administrators disconnected from corporate management. Additionally, investor-owned hospitals competed for patients and doctors even if they were in the same city and owned by the same company. In retrospect, such a strategy seems incongruous. Yet, it fit the logic of how Wall Street-backed companies operate: living and dying by the quarterly earnings report. The emphasis on quarterly earnings is pushed down to the hospital level and is underscored in the compensation packages for local administrators.

Traditionally, administrators' bonuses were tied to specific hospital performance, not to the city, or even regional, system. Helping a sister hospital across town might help the company, but to an individual hospital CEO, that was irrelevant at bonus time. Columbia shifted the paradigm. Bonuses hinged on an overall market's financial results, not just a single hospital. Looking at the market in its entirety also provided a big-picture strategy to the entire healthcare system in the region. Under this structure, market managers could appropriately buy surgery centers, home care agencies, or assisted-living centers to fill in the gaps in the healthcare continuum.

Actually, large not-for-profit systems have operated that way for years. For example, consider Baptist Memorial Hospital in Memphis and its network of hospitals, rehabilitation centers, outpatient centers, fitness club, and day-care center. For the first time, a tax-paying system, Columbia, was incorporating that strategy into its own plan, and it proved to be a propitious and profitable one.

Scott instilled his business principles in Columbia market managers and hospital CEOs. Each CEO received a copy of the book, *Customers for Life,* by Carl Sewell, a Cadillac dealer in Dallas. Sewell, a meticulous manager concerned about customers' perceptions of quality, built his car lot into a $250 million business. The book includes an entire chapter on rest rooms, for instance. "He says take care of your customers," Scott said of Sewell and his philosophy, adding, "If you do, they're going to be customers for life."

By 1990, Columbia owned 11 hospitals with revenues of $290 million. Profits were a mere $9 million, but Scott was already reporting what would become an industry standard (and Columbia's favorite acronym): earnings before depreciation, interest, taxes, and amortization (EBDITA). EBDITA shows a company's cash flow. In essence it is a financial ratio that other industries use to report how their cash flow is improving or diminishing. For example, Columbia reported that the EBDITA generated in El Paso soared upwards from $8.4 million to $40 million in four years.

Meanwhile, in Fort Worth, such financial ratios and other details of proposed deals were sketched out with colorful markers from floor to ceiling on Scott's white, vinyl walls. He closely followed stock quotes and stories on his computer and incessantly called physicians and hospital administrators to find hospitals to buy.

In May 1990 Scott had another tool in his financial arsenal, publicly traded stock. Columbia went public through a merger with Smith Laboratories, a San Diego–based medical equipment firm. In keeping with Scott's nature, the merger was actually a frugal way of becoming a publicly traded firm. As an added bonus from the arrangement, he gained $39 million in Smith Lab's cash reserves in the process. Scott frequently criticized the million-dollar fees paid to bankers and lawyers by hospital chains. This merger with Smith Labs was a way to go public and escape a lot of that "wasteful" expense.

Once Columbia was a publicly traded firm, Scott worked hard at meeting the expectations of Wall Street's high-powered stock analysts. Yet his words often fell on deaf ears. "It was a small company and people ignored it," recalled Jeff Putterman, formerly an analyst at Stephens, an investment banking firm in Little Rock, Arkansas. "Also, other people in the industry belittled it," Putterman noted.

Correspondingly, some Republic Health Corporation executives privately were accusing Scott of ripping off their company's strategy of physician partnerships. Columbia and Republic were about the same size at that time—medium-sized companies that garnered little attention in the stock market. Stock analysts were paid to research stocks with large shareholder followings, such as NME and AMI. Yet, those who knew Scott saw the momentum building. He wasn't waiting for Wall Street to catch up. "I'm extremely impatient and I try to be results oriented," he explained. In July 1990 Columbia began building its south Texas network, buying HEI, a Houston-based three-hospital chain, for $22 million.

One of Scott's missteps also came in 1990 when he bought Willow Creek Adolescent Center in Arlington, Texas, for $9.4 million in cash and $3 million in assumed debt. Nine administrators later, Columbia sold it to the not-for-profit Adventist system. Remarkably, Willow Creeks's fortunes improved considerably. Administrator Don Sykes said employees threw him a party on his seven-month anniversary with the hospital. (No Columbia administrator had lasted seven months before his arrival.) That type of turnover illustrates the impatience Columbia often had for hospital CEOs who did not produce expected results.

FUNDAMENTALLY, A FINANCIAL WHIZ

Not every deal would go Columbia's way, but one thing was certain: Scott seemed to excel at raising capital. In March 1992 Columbia sold $100 million in bonds and then in June sold another $135 million to buy Basic American Medical and two AMI hospitals in Houston for $35 million. By this time, Columbia was named the nation's 12th fastest-growing public company by *Fortune* magazine.

Yet the big transactions, the billion-dollar deals, were still around the corner. One day, Stephens's investment banker, Putterman, called Scott and said, "Why don't you ever go to Europe?" "Nobody's ever invited us to go to Europe," was Scott's answer. Soon the two were jetting across the Atlantic, and Stephens hosted a European road show to introduce Scott to investors over there. "Every time I met with Rick, I came away thinking he was smarter than the time before," Putterman said. Scott was learning from some of the best. One of his smartest moves, he says, was hiring a few men from Methodist Hospital in Houston, including Columbia/HCA's former CFO David Colby.

Methodist was rich and successful throughout the late 1980s and early 1990s. Thanks to sizable Medicare reimbursements and relatively few charity care write-offs, the 1,500-bed hospital racked up nearly $1 billion in cash reserves by 1996. In fact, Methodist was the most profitable hospital in the country in 1991, with $76 million in profits on revenues of $526 million, according to Healthcare Investment Analysts (HCIA), a

Baltimore-based research firm. The credit for Methodist's stellar performance went to President and CEO, Larry Mathis, a brash Texan who ran the hospital like the multimillion-dollar business it was. His management style was so indelibly imprinted on Methodist that some referred to the hospital as "Mathodist."

After agreeing to buy the El Paso hospitals in early 1988, Scott hired two Methodist executives, Russell Schneider and Ruben Perez, to be CEO and CFO, respectively, of Columbia's first two hospitals. Both went out to El Paso in April, yet Schneider stayed in touch with Colby, who was CFO of Methodist. The two men had worked together on an especially difficult financing deal for San Jacinto Methodist Hospital, and they respected each other's abilities.

One weekend, Colby went out to help Schneider with Columbia's new El Paso operations. "I didn't make any big secret about it," Colby said. When Mathis found out, he gave Colby an ultimatum. Either stop helping Schneider or stop being CFO of one of the nation's largest and most profitable hospitals. "I'm going to help Russ," Colby answered. He quit Methodist, took one day off, and started the next day for Columbia.

Hiring top executives away from not-for-profit hospitals wasn't the custom among investor-owned chains. They usually recruited from other for-profit companies or "grew their own," as Humana did, by hiring future managers straight out of graduate school. Still, not-for-profit hospitals are obviously full of strong profit-minded executives. Even though they're called "not-for-profit," over the years these tax-exempt hospitals have been more profitable than their for-profit counterparts. In 1990, for example, for-profit hospitals posted a median total profit margin of 2.5 percent compared with 3.2 percent for not-for-profit facilities, HCIA reported.

The profitability statistic didn't invert until 1992 when investor-owned hospitals reported a 4.5 percent total profit ratio compared to 4.1 percent for not-for-profit organizations. Notably, the gap widened in 1993 when taxpaying hospitals demonstrated a 5.6 percent margin versus 4.2 percent for their tax-exempt counterparts.

With the Columbia era, the profitability of investor-owned hospitals became even greater. They were performing between three and four times better than the industry overall. While only 19% of the industry was logging double-digit profit margins in 1995, 38% of for-profit hospitals were achieving double-digit profit margins— music to investors' ears.

As it grew, Columbia began to change from a regional hospital chain to a national one. Even so, most of the management team remained intact. For example, David Vandewater, who started as Columbia's COO in 1991, worked side by side with Scott right up to the day the two men were forced to resign in July 1997. Vandewater met Scott through Republic Health Corporation, where Vandewater was COO. Vandewater was very familiar with Columbia's first investment in El Paso, as his first hospital job was running Vista Hills Medical Center (located in El Paso) from 1979 to 1982. Coincidentally, Columbia bought Vista Hills in the summer of 1988. Vandewater joined Columbia in July 1990 as senior vice president of operations. At the time, Vandewater acknowledged he was taking a cut in pay from his $300,000-plus salary at Republic. (He would later be handsomely rewarded for his compensation backslide.)

Vandewater remained the number-two man behind Scott through all the subsequent mergers. In late 1993, Scott gave Vandewater 109,237 shares of Columbia, worth approximately $3 million. The transaction was an unusual one—a personal transfer of wealth from Scott to Vandewater to thank him for his work in building Columbia.

It's not surprising that Scott's inner circle remained the same while the company grew dramatically in the past few years. "He knows exactly who his friends were when nobody else was paying attention," said investment banker Putterman. In fact, Putterman notes that his firm, Stephens, was retained to advise Columbia when it was merging with Galen in 1993. This seemed to be an odd move since the Little Rock firm is hardly a Wall Street luminary, such as say, Merrill Lynch or Donaldson Lufkin & Jenrette. Yet Scott stayed loyal and gave Stephens the business and a $1.5 million fee, which sounds exorbitant, but is a pittance in Wall Street terms. Galen's adviser, Goldman Sachs in New York, collected $8 million for its advice in the $3.2 billion merger.

Most hospital chain executives didn't blink at the prospect of such fees. Back in 1986, Donaldson Lufkin & Jenrette, another Wall Street investment bank, collected $10 million to advise Scott's former legal client, Republic, in its $800 million leveraged buyout. Despite the high-priced advice, that deal turned decidedly sour as Republic ended up in bankruptcy reorganization. However, the Galen merger sailed along and launched Columbia into the big time. Galen was four times the size of Columbia, bulking up Columbia's once sleek organization.

Up until then, Scott had articulated a simple strategy of expanding the company one market at a time. However, that strategy went out the window when logic dictated another course. Scott had a paperweight on his desk in Louisville that read, "If you are not the lead dog, the view never changes." What helped Scott move into the lead was a shift among the other "dogs," most notably Humana.

THE GALEN ACQUISITION

Enrollment in Humana's insurance health plan (Humana Care Plus) peaked in 1991 at about 1.7 million. Additionally, Humana's reputation was starting to sag. Self-promoted as the low-cost providers, Humana's hospitals were being branded as the high-markup providers. An *ABC News* report in 1991 slammed the chain for its mark-ups, citing a 60-cent thermometer for which Humana had charged $11.80. Shortly after that occurrence, the Inspector General of the U.S. Department of Health and Human Services initiated an investigation into Humana's Medicare cost reports.

As Humana's star dimmed with the public, the company suffered another crucial blow. In 1991, Wendell Cherry, widely regarded as the company's visionary, died of cancer. The following year, Jones proposed to split the company into an insurance company called Humana and a hospital company called Galen Healthcare (Galen), named for a Greek physician regarded as one of the fathers of medicine.

The move was prompted by the realization that mixing insurance and hospitals was not working. Physicians in some cities, such as San Antonio, rebelled against Humana's managed care plan. In retaliation, they began referring their patients to non-Humana hospitals. Meanwhile, health plans and HMOs that competed with Humana Care Plus didn't want to give any business to Humana hospitals. Humana was burning the candle at both ends.

In the division that ensued, Humana founder David Jones kept the insurance side, which would retain the Humana name. Two long-time Humana executives, Carl Pollard and Jim Bohanon, were named to head the hospital company, Galen.

In March of 1993, Columbia bought a Galen hospital in Beaumont, Texas, and in the midst of talking about other deals, Scott broached the subject of merging with Galen. The deal was simple. Pollard wanted to protect the former Humana employees, so he insisted the merged company be based in his hometown of Louisville. Yet he basically turned over the reins to the younger and ever-energetic Scott and his team. Bohanon shared COO duties with Vandewater, but only for a few months, at which time Bohanon, a paraplegic with health problems, retired.

The merger with Galen strengthened Columbia's networks in Fort Lauderdale, Houston, and Corpus Christi. Florida was especially important, and soon the company would cover the state like a blanket. (Now, 95 percent of Floridians are within a 20-minute drive of a Columbia/HCA hospital.)

"When Columbia first came to the market, nobody took them seriously," said Miami attorney Sandra Greenblatt. "They were buying hospitals that had never been a competitive threat." That's because in Florida, Columbia started with another castoff. When Scott bought 300-bed Victoria in December 1988, it was nearly insolvent, losing $400,000 a month. Citicorp anted up again with $17 million, and Scott went into business with 85 local physicians who also purchased equity in the hospital; their individual investments ranged from $20,000 to $30,000. Nine physicians were elected to a Medical Executive Council that met once a week to discuss hospital management. Within a year, the hospital was making money again.

In 1992 Scott bought Basic American Medical, a small Indianapolis-based chain for $185 million in cash and stock. Basic—known as "bammy" for its stock symbol, BAMI—derived 80 percent of its profits from a four-hospital network in the Fort Lauderdale area. BAMI's founders had pledged their shares to repay a loan to Marriott and needed to sell. Scott proved to be the white knight they needed.

Through a series of mergers and acquisitions, Columbia grew like kudzu in Florida. "We put down a list of hospitals we wanted to buy," said Vandewater in early 1994, adding, "We've got them." Columbia executives wooed area physicians at a Columbia-sponsored party at St. Petersburg's ThunderDome stadium. To the musical strains of a Miami band, the Pink Flamingos, the event cost an estimated $20,000.

THE UBIQUITOUS COLUMBIA

With hospitals and physicians falling in line on a grand scale, Scott was playing a tune that Wall Street loved. The lyrics read, "rapid consolidation of a large and fragmented market." In healthcare, that consolidation was happening in a variety of niches: home healthcare, surgery centers, physician groups, and ambulance services. But no other niche carried the clout, the dollars, and the potential for profits as the hospital industry. Suddenly, Columbia seemed to be talking to everyone. The standing joke among hospital administrators was, "Have you gotten an acquisition offer from Columbia yet? It's the letter that starts out, *Dear Occupant.*"

In city after city, Columbia's acquisition and regional man-agers pressed forward. They would contact doctors, trustees, and hospital CEOs about selling all or part of their hospitals. They'd send out letters with news clippings about Columbia's latest deals. In Columbia's 1993 annual report, Scott predicted what would happen in 1994. "The shake out has begun, reform is happening and Columbia/HCA Healthcare—not only will we survive, we are positioned to excel." Indeed, 1994 was to be a banner year for Columbia. It started in February with the $7.6 billion merger/acquisition of HCA, giving Scott and his team control of a $10 billion corporation. "I sought Rick out," Thomas Frist Jr. noted, in discussing how the merger came about.

However, what Frist never explained was that he was about to radically restructure HCA after he read a copy of the Clinton health plan. Clinton's plan proposed purchasing alliances that would contract with provider networks for care. Columbia's strategy to form networks in local markets made sense to Frist, and he saw it as the future.

Interestingly, Frist's plan to radically revamp HCA was never reported. Frist had planned to convert all of HCA's 100 hospitals to tax-exempt institutions. "I was going to convert six billion dollars in assets and take it off the tax rolls," Frist said later about his grand plan. Goldman Sachs, a Wall Street investment banking firm, was lined up to issue bonds. Frist's plan was to convert all of the hospitals to tax-exempt corporations, but HCA would continue to manage them. Under the new structure, the hospitals could issue tax-exempt bonds, which would be cheaper. Yet Frist saw a new opportunity with Scott. "Rather than predict the future, you could create the future," he said, regarding his eventual decision to team up with the burgeoning Columbia organization.

Even so, it's curious to think what might have happened had Frist gone ahead with his plan. If HCA had converted all of its hospitals to tax-exempt ones, would other investor-owned chains have followed? As mentioned earlier in the book, the hospital industry is often accused of having a "herd" mentality. It's highly likely that other systems would have followed HCA's lead. What would that have done to the tax base of the involved communities? Another consideration is whether HCA's move would have led to the demise of the investor-owned hospital sector. No one will know how the market would have reacted to such a dramatic action, but the fact that he considered such a move demonstrates that Frist thinks big, and he plans ahead for a variety of contingencies. Referring to the plan to convert HCA's hospitals, he commented, "That's the type of contingency plan that's always going on."

This was one contingency plan that remained untested (and largely unknown). Instead, Frist called Richard Rainwater, who was Scott's partner in starting Columbia. Frist had become friends with Rainwater, who had invested in HCA's leveraged buyout in 1988. Frist noted that "Rainwater kept telling me about Rick Scott, and how great he was, and I kept blowing it off." Apparently by 1993, the time was right to heed Rainwater's repeated calls. With the merger, HCA's operations were now in Scott's hands. Frist became chairman, but Scott was "the boss." Two other large mergers followed the HCA alliance. In September, Columbia/HCA bought Medical Care America, the nation's largest outpatient surgery chain, in an $850 million acquisition.

Medical Care America, a Dallas-based outpatient surgery center company, had been fed on the demands of disgruntled doctors. It opened several surgery centers across the street from Humana hospitals. How was it able to accomplish such a tactic? Fundamentally, Humana had upset its doctors with the Humana Care Plus health plan, which scrutinized their admissions and in some cases, capitated their payments. Humana and its physicians became enemies in a handful of cities, and to "exact revenge," some of those doctors took their surgery business elsewhere.

Therefore, when Columbia bought Medical Care America, the deal fit like a glove because Columbia had acquired all of the former Humana hospitals. Then later, in 1994 Columbia initiated the move to merge with HealthTrust. "It's unlikely I'm going to do anything without Tommy's input," Scott said, when completing the merger with HCA. What the world didn't know was that Frist and Scott were already working together on Clayton McWhorter, chairman, president, and CEO of HealthTrust. In fact, Frist would be pivotal to Scott's dogged persistence in acquiring HealthTrust, which was being heavily wooed by NME at the same time.

In January of 1994, one month before the HCA merger was completed, Frist and Scott were already talking to McWhorter about a possible deal. Talks initially had centered around some possible joint ventures or asset swaps, but neither proposition looked good to McWhorter. "Asset swaps are difficult because everyone thinks their assets are worth more," McWhorter said. A joint venture between a Columbia hospital and a HealthTrust facility invariably would put the HealthTrust hospital in a minority position, which wasn't acceptable either.

Talk about a larger deal waned while McWhorter worked to finish HealthTrust's $1 billion purchase of Epic. However, right after that closed in May, Frist and Scott came hounding again. Scott accused McWhorter of procrastinating. "Rick would talk about a price. I would say it's not good enough. Go away," McWhorter recalled.

In early August, McWhorter heard from a new suitor, former investment banker, Jeffrey Barbakow. Barbakow took over NME in 1993 when the company was mired in fraud allegations surrounding its psychiatric hospitals. Barbakow's job was to turn around the Santa Monica, California–based chain, a feat he accomplished. Barbakow proposed a new tactic: merge HealthTrust with NME and AMI, whose majority owners were looking for a way to cash out. McWhorter agreed to talk, although he was skeptical about whether a final offer would be high enough. Even so, he signed confidentiality agreements with AMI and NME, the first step toward a possible deal.

By the end of the month, however, Frist and Scott were at the door again, wanting a deal, which provides some insight into how Columbia completed so many megadeals in just a few years: persistence. Scott and Frist's dogged pursuit of HealthTrust is but one example. Scott and his lieutenants focused on the end goal: getting the deal done. Then, they gritted it out. Their determination to do the deal did not wane.

NME LOSES HEALTHTRUST TO COLUMBIA

In September of 1994, a draft of Barbakow's speech announcing a merger between NME, AMI, and HealthTrust at the annual shareholders' meeting was leaked by a disgruntled employee to *The Wall Street Journal*. It became the biggest whodunit in the hospital industry. Who leaked the speech and why? Was the merger going to happen?

While the industry was abuzz with news of a possible triumvirate of NME, AMI, and HealthTrust, Scott and Frist persisted. "Rick's not going to let that happen," said one senior Columbia official when asked about NME's possible deal. This senior official was right.

On September 29, McWhorter held an executive committee meeting at 3 P.M., followed by a board meeting at 5 P.M. He had three options: stay independent, merge with NME and AMI, or merge with Columbia. He considered the numbers and the options and was going to recommend staying independent.

At 2 P.M., Scott and Frist called to up their bid, and it was enough. McWhorter walked into the executive committee meeting and recommended the Columbia option. At 5 P.M., the board voted to go with Columbia. Four days later, NME returned with a counterproposal, but McWhorter said it still wasn't good enough. HealthTrust stayed with Columbia.

On October 4, 1994, there was a conference call to announce the HealthTrust deal. On the line were 300 of Columbia's closest followers: Wall Street investment bankers and analysts. (This was quite a change from the days when Columbia couldn't get analysts to write about the company. Now they were fawning all over the healthcare giant.) All the power brokers were there: Scott, McWhorter, Vandewater, and Frist. Ed Gordon from Morgan Stanley, a New York–based investment banking firm was the host. The mood was jovial. Scott introduced everyone, naming Vandewater as "the guy who's going to have to pull this whole thing together." He introduced McWhorter as the company's new chairman, adding that Frist, the former chairman, would now be the vice chairman. Scott joked that "If you're chairman of the board of this company, your longevity is only about six months." McWhorter and Frist were together again.

Putting together billion-dollar deals like Columbia and HCA, and Columbia/HCA and HealthTrust, takes financial talent—the money has to be right. The chemistry among personalities must be right also. McWhorter and Frist are two guys who can finish each other's sentences. In retrospect, it almost seems ludicrous to think McWhorter would have done a deal with the Californians and New York bankers who run NME.

McWhorter joked that the merger was "an opportunity to rejoin Tommy after being kicked out of the big house and into the condo." He was, of course, referring to HealthTrust's split from HCA. There's more than a little truth to his jibe. As noted earlier, administrators at HealthTrust hospitals sometimes felt like stepchildren to HCA executives, and relations between the two camps were often tinged with rivalry. With HealthTrust snapped from its grasp, NME, led by Jeffrey Barbakow, was forced to settle for AMI alone. Although Barbakow touted the AMI deal as the best one ever, one Wall Street analyst, Todd Richter, called it an "ego-driven deal. It makes the buyer bigger but not better."

In contrast, analysts loved the prospects of HealthTrust's hospitals joining Columbia, a company run by the 40-something crowd. However, McWhorter and Frist added balance from another generation, now regarded as the industry's "gray hairs," as did Donald MacNaughton, a HealthTrust director and longtime HCA executive who was elected to Columbia's board. MacNaughton was 77 and had been a mentor to McWhorter, age 61.

Following a conference call on the Columbia/HCA–HealthTrust merger, MacNaughton talked privately to McWhorter. "You have a problem," he said, flatly. Then he told McWhorter that he had a tendency to talk too long and that Columbia's president and CEO, Scott, was "going to turn McWhorter off," meaning that at some point Scott might simply stop listening.

McWhorter laughed and agreed that sometimes he did tend to go on and on in his quest to make a point. He pledged to be quick and concise in his points, especially when talking with Scott, who was naturally impatient. "What I admire most about Don MacNaughton is he tells you what you need to know," McWhorter said.

Columbia now had the men who helped build the investor-owned industry on its board. MacNaughton, Frist, and McWhorter would watch and counsel, but the torch had been passed to Scott, who, at this point, appeared to be the race's swiftest runner.

COLUMBIA'S EXPERIENCE WITH NOT-FOR-PROFIT HOSPITALS

If Columbia were just buying other for-profit hospitals, that would have been one thing. However, Columbia was crossing the tracks and buying not-for-profit hospitals.

"When tax-exempt hospitals look around for a merger partner, I'm the logical person to do business with," Scott said. By selling to Columbia, not-for-profit hospitals could join a network and get 30 percent better prices on medical supplies. That's better than the buying groups of not-for-profit hospitals, Scott argued. He added that proceeds from the sale of a tax-exempt facility to Columbia/HCA (usually in the tens of millions of dollars) could fund a host of charitable endeavors in the community.

There are those who questioned whether Columbia's pricing was indeed 30 percent better, while others wondered if a foundation was better than a tax-exempt hospital. Even so, Scott's arguments were apparently working. In 1994, not a month went by that a not-for-profit hospital wasn't selling out to Columbia or another publicly traded system (a Columbia "wanna-be"). Indeed, Scott was bringing a mob of emulators with him—aggressive "Pac-man" capitalists chomping to toss cash toward hospital-selling, tax-exempt boards. It wasn't as easy as Scott made it look, however. "Why can't these tax-

exempt people make a decision?" other investor-owned executives complained.

No investor-owned chain purchased more not-for-profit hospitals than Columbia, which ironically, Scott did while irritating
the not-for-profit hospitals as a group. He and his top executives
began publicly questioning the tax-exempt hospitals' very reason for being: their mission as a charitable, tax-exempt organization. Scott and his followers believed that hospitals should
pay taxes or provide a level of indigent care that makes up for
the lack of tax payments. In his mind, it was that simple. Early
on, Scott and Vandewater were clear about how they viewed not-
for-profit hospitals. If an individual said "not-for-profit," they immediately corrected him or her. "Tax-exempt," was their corrective reply.

By 1994 the rhetoric was even stronger. "They're not 'not-
for-profit,' they're 'non-taxpaying'" was how Columbia's new executives labeled them. The distinction investor-owned executives made is clear. From their perspective, profits aren't the
dividing line between the two classes of hospitals; taxes are.
Some facilities pay them; others don't. That's how the two
species differ, they reasoned.

"Non-taxpaying hospitals shouldn't be in business. They're
not good corporate citizens," Columbia's Scott said in a 1994
Washington Post interview. This quote heard round the healthcare world became a rallying cry for not-for-profit hospital executives. "See? I told you this guy was out to get us," they clamored.

Scott contended that his words were taken out of context.
In a letter to the *Post,* he wrote: "My comments were focused on
the fact that the premise for which non-taxpaying hospitals was
established no longer existed, particularly if universal coverage
becomes a reality." Still, nothing really stirred up Scott or his
managers more than talking about the labels that historically
have described the two distinctions of hospitals. "If we're for-
profit, are they for-loss?" Scott asked.

Predictably, Columbia has been accused of playing hardball
against tax-exempt hospitals on the issue of taxes. In 1993, the
company won a contract away from Lee Memorial Hospital in

Fort Myers, Florida, after releasing a study that showed that Lee Memorial was making money on its tax exemption. The study revealed that Lee Memorial was exempted from $10 million in taxes, while only providing $4 million in charity care. That amounted to a $6 million profit on its tax exemption, Columbia charged.

Lee Memorial executives disputed the figures, saying they provided $12 million in charity care and received less than $6 million in tax breaks. Despite the disparity in figures, Columbia won the $7 million contract to provide care to the county's employees.

The Lee case wasn't the end of it, though. The Hospital Alliance of Tennessee volleyed back with a study showing that the state's not-for-profit hospitals provided between 87 and 99 percent of the charity care in their communities. "Who's in control of your healthcare—Wall Street or Main Street?" asked Elliott Moore, the group's president. "Offers by investor-owned suitors will pale when community leaders understand the benefits of the not-for-profit's commitment to its neighbors and the importance of local control of the services it provides," Moore added.

"Very definitely, there is a stronger division among for-profits and not-for-profits," said John Bozard, vice president for strategic development at Orlando Regional Heathcare System in 1994 after Columbia announced its proposed merger with HealthTrust. Orlando Regional had a joint venture with HealthTrust, but Bozard said that would end with the Columbia merger. "Columbia is a competitor," he maintained, noting the four Columbia hospitals in his region.

The tax status controversy swelled as Columbia pollinated Scott's ideas and funding among the not-for-profit ranks, creating a growing maelstrom of emotions between the tax-exempt and the taxpaying. By 1995 Catholic leaders also were feeling pressure to speak out. "Not-for-profit healthcare organizations are better suited than their investor-owned counterparts to support the patient-first ethic in medicine," said the late Cardinal Joseph Bernardin in his address to Chicago's business leaders in a speech entitled, "Making the Case for Not-for-Profit Healthcare," in January 1995. "Especially in light of capitation—when providers are at financial risk—the people must ensure that the nation not convert to a predominantly investor-owned delivery system," Bernardin warned.

He warned of "the rougher edges of capitalism's inclination toward excessive individualism," and that the "not-for-profit sector in healthcare may already be eroding as a result of today's extremely turbulent competitive environment in healthcare." Notably, these comments came right after three not-for-profit hospitals in Chicago were sold to Columbia. This was hardly a landslide, but an erosion looked like it might be under way. Since its acquisition spree began seven years earlier, Columbia had bought hospitals of all religions. It bought a Catholic facility in Fort Worth, Texas and one owned by the Reorganized Church of Jesus Christ of Latter Day Saints in Independence, Missouri; and it merged a Catholic and a Jewish hospital in Miami.

By 1994, other for-profit systems were following the Columbia lead. AMI bought St. Francis Hospital in Memphis, Tennessee, for $92 million. Health Management Associates bought Holy Name of Jesus Medical Center in Gadsden, Alabama. Notably, the number of Catholic hospitals fell from 624 in 1988 to 581 in 1993, according to Catholic Health Association. Scott believed the decline would continue: "It's just logical. Their mission was to take care of charity patients. That mission has passed."

It's interesting how quickly longtime executives at not-for-profit hospitals seemed to change their tune, once they were employed by Columbia. In early 1994, James Pickle, president and CEO of Erlanger Medical Center in Chattanooga, Tennessee, was hired to run Columbia's Louisville hospital network. Despite his tax-exempt roots, Pickle indicted other not-for-profit hospitals in Chattanooga, saying that Erlanger—the city's tax-supported public hospital—shouldered nearly all of the city's indigent care. The other not-for-profit hospitals in town provided "virtually no charity care," he stated. He further argued that continued tax-exempt status for not-for-profit hospitals was "questionable."

Scott contended that many other public hospital executives agreed. He backed up his premise, citing Columbia's acquisition of tax-exempt hospitals in Florida that provided no charity care. Nearly all of the patients were elderly and covered by Medicare, he explained.

"You're misleading people to say hospitals like Methodist are not-for-profit. It's a joke. They're tax-exempt," said Taylor Boone, who chaired Southwest Texas Methodist Hospital in San Antonio. Methodist agreed to a 50–50 joint venture with Columbia in the early part of 1995 that converted the hospital's tax status to taxpaying and fed about $20 million into a new Methodist foundation. "Methodist has never been 'not for profit,'" he noted, adding that, "it's always made millions of dollars a year in profits." At the time, Boone predicted more tax-exempt hospitals would sell out to chains. "Some have been part of the problem in healthcare," he said, adding that the system had become lazy about finding cost-effective ways of delivering care.

Scott promoted cost-effectiveness, but he also stressed quality, which was a hard characteristic to measure. He tied the two together, noting that these concepts of quality and cost are mutually consistent. This flew in the face of critics, who charged that cutting costs would impair quality. "The fact is, our quality is better and our satisfaction is better" after consolidations, Scott said. "We would like to do everything we can to consolidate the excess capacity in the industry."

Scott knew that cost was only one factor in his quest to change the industry. Quality, that elusive mark of distinction, was equally important. That's why Columbia excelled at getting the highest marks from the only group that awards quality ratings to hospitals, the Joint Commission on the Accreditation of Healthcare Organizations. All of Columbia's hospitals were Joint Commission accredited, and 21 percent of its hospitals received accreditation with commendation, the organization's highest honor. Nationally, only 12 percent of hospitals receive it, Columbia pointed out.

It also advertised the fact that a disproportionate share of its hospitals made the industry's top 100 list. In 1995 it had 29;

in 1996 it had 17. These were pretty good percentages for a company that had only six percent of the nation's hospitals. (The top 100 list is compiled by HCIA and the Health Care Provider Consulting Practice of William M. Mercer, a human resources management firm based in New York. Its standards include financial management, operations, and clinical practices.)

Scott's frugality wasn't imposed only on others, however. It also carried over to the management suite. Columbia wasn't known for paying the industry's top salaries. Scott figured that talented executives would flock to the company just for the experience and notation on their resumes. For the most part, he was right. In this age of consolidation, dozens of Columbia executives used their experience to get jobs with consolidators in other healthcare niches.

Scott allowed himself no special dispensations in this area, keeping with his distaste of excess. Scott's office in Nashville was extremely modest and certainly not the largest in the company. He had just a desk and a table for meetings, a laptop on his paper-cluttered desk, and family photos on the shelves. For years, Scott earned a salary that was much less than many not-for-profit health system CEOs. Not only had his salary been smaller, but his bureaucracy of high-paid executives was thinner. Scott's 1995 salary and bonus was $1.5 million. In comparison the chairman and CEO of Citicorp, a company of similar financial size, received a salary and bonus of $3.5 million in 1996, and three vice chairman earned more than $1 million in salary and bonuses.

In spite of its pay scale, Columbia's history of creating wealth for its management was a major draw. Long-time managers of HCA and HealthTrust, two hospital chains that were absorbed into Columbia, left eventually as multimillionaires thanks to company stock programs. Even the rank and file had a chance for future wealth, albeit not in the millions of dollars. Employees could purchase stock through payroll deduction at a 15 percent discount to the market, which is fairly typical for a publicly held corporation.

Competitors hated the fact that Scott touted his hospitals' quality ratings. Bragging about such things was viewed as uncouth. Yet in person, Scott wasn't a cocky or rude individual. He was unquestionably polite. However, his tendency to say what he thought, coupled with Columbia's monolithic size, made his opinions larger than life. This velocity of exposure and expectation can be a detriment. "You don't need to get people bowed up and coming together to depose you," McWhorter commented about Scott. For example, in Houston one source said the new strategy among tax-exempt hospitals was "ABC— Anybody but Columbia."

Columbia certainly left some disgruntled civic boosters in Louisville. When Scott pulled the company's headquarters out 10 months after pledging to stay, locals bad-mouthed him. John Ed Pearce, a columnist for the *Louisville Courier-Journal,* called him "Slick Rick," adding, "His heart is on business and is hardened toward civic duties and such. He loves not your city but what he can get from it." Scott yanked 600 jobs from Louisville, dashing the city's hopes of becoming a healthcare capital, when he moved the company to Nashville. In his defense, Columbia executives claimed the state of Kentucky had not kept its promise to repeal certain taxes on hospitals.

Conversely, another Louisville columnist, Linda Raymond, reported these insightful comments from University of Louisville associate economics professor, Paul A. Coomes. "Too few business students expect to become entrepreneurs, building a company the way Scott did. After they get their business degrees, they expect someone to hand them a job and a paycheck," Coomes noted. "Scott was a wonderful role model for young people," he added, claiming that he was "a walking, talking, moneymaking example of what Junior Achievement teaches."

Scott was a capitalist and an entrepreneur whose talents were both admired and vilified. He had built a company from nothing—a true entrepreneur. He believed hospitals were businesses, and he believed they should pay taxes. Yet many began to question whether size would become an asset or a liability for Columbia. Largeness may lower overhead costs, but it began to raise other less tangible costs. Columbia became the "Big Corporate Entity" in a business that can be very personal and emotional. When Columbia wanted to close a hospital in Destin, Florida, because it already owned a hospital in nearby Fort Walton Beach, the company was portrayed as an unfeeling monolith. "I think the city is being betrayed," Destin City Councilman Chester Kroeger told *Northwest Florida Daily News.* "We don't want Columbia/HCA in our community anymore."

Under pressure from the state to keep the hospital open by selling it to another buyer, Columbia/HCA agreed to sell it to HMD Healthcare Corporation, out of St. Petersburg, Florida. Coincidentally, HMD's president, Scott L. Hopes, was registered as a lobbyist for Columbia in 1992 when he testified before the Florida Legislature on behalf of a Columbia-commissioned study on physician practice patterns.

Largeness also has disadvantages in getting scores of executives to sing off the same sheet of music. Early in 1995, *Chicago Sun-Times* reporter Della de Lafuente heard from a source that Columbia was interested in buying University of Chicago Hospitals, a powerful 609-bed system. Columbia executives had spoken frequently of pursuing medical school hospitals, and for that reason, the rumor sounded sensible, except for one aspect: Columbia already had a relationship with a medical school, University of Illinois, through the chain's largest Chicago facility, Michael Reese Hospital. Still, the source backed up the rumor, saying that Robert Galloway, a Columbia vice president, had mentioned a University of Chicago deal in the works during a seminar in Florida. Galloway had spoken at Interhealth, a conference for church-related health systems.

Since most conferences sell cassette tapes of those sessions, de Lafuente called the conference and ordered the tapes of Galloway's session. Sure enough, Galloway mentioned that Columbia either had or was pursuing relationships with five teaching hospitals, and the University of Chicago was one of them. "This would be really big news here," the healthcare business reporter said. "I've got everyone in town looking into this." The implications were huge. If Columbia bought University of Chicago Hospitals, the chain might not need Michael Reese.

Considering Columbia's consolidation philosophy, maybe it would shut the hospital down. The obvious question arose, "How many jobs would be lost?"

Sam Holtzman, who managed the Chicago market for Columbia, finally called back after a few days. "No, no, no," he said. "Galloway doesn't know what we're doing here in Chicago. He just got mixed up because he didn't know the difference between University of Chicago and University of Illinois." That type of confusion could accelerate in a company moving at Mach speed and filled with a mix of corporate cultures.

In fact, some pundits questioned whether Columbia was growing too fast to keep its own operations moving smoothly. "At some point in time, you have to attend to the business," said Robert O'Leary, who formerly headed AMI, Dallas-based hospital chain.

Nonetheless, Columbia's chairman McWhorter was with HCA during its height and said after the HealthTrust merger that Columbia would hold confusion to a minimum by keeping its management structure flat. "You have to be careful about layers," McWhorter said. He further acknowledged that the tough part of a growing company is actually running it. "It's not fun being a captive in your office," McWhorter noted. "It's more fun doing deals and visiting hospitals."

For the myriad healthcare professionals and advisers faced with the daily dilemma of how to deal with the industry giant, fun was not likely a word associated with Columbia. And, for those who were called on to carry out Columbia's ambitious growth goals; well, they were not having much fun either.

3

CHAPTER

Healthcare Has Never Worked Like This Before

Be daring. Be first. Be different.
Rick Scott

BRANDING TO THE MAX

Of all the tactics undertaken by Columbia management, none was as visible and universal as the branding campaign. The concept came out of the notion that Columbia "needed to become a household word—one as familiar as Kellogg's and Campbell's Soup." However, from the outset the idea had as many opponents as proponents, the latter camp being led by Rick Scott and his senior vice president of marketing, Lindy Richardson. Scott had said that "by establishing a name and brand identity, we will establish our services in the eyes of the consumer as the ones to choose."

As for detractors, there was no shortage. Among the unimpressed was Tommy Frist Jr., who would eventually cut the campaign the same day he took over the reins of Columbia/HCA. On a conference call to company executives he stated, "if you call headquarters next Monday and you hear some kind of catchy Columbia ad, then you'll know I'm not doing my job." Less than a week after Scott's departure, Frist revealed to the *St. Petersburg Times* his true feeling regarding the campaign: "I've thought those ads were too cutesy for the past two years. We're not Bud Light or Coors. We're a healthcare giver and you can bet our competitors' ads are going to be all warm and fuzzy. Our ads never sat right with me."

Actually, the ads never sat right with a fair number of folks, and part of that was by design. The Columbia marketing team wanted to develop a campaign that would be memorable and out of the ordinary. Their main objective was to increase awareness of the Columbia name, which, when the campaign started, was less than five percent "unaided awareness." Unaided awareness is the term market researchers use to measure a company's name without any prompting. As the marketing group had noted, "Columbia is the nation's leading provider. However, research shows that most Americans don't even know the name."

The idea behind increasing awareness was that if people knew about all the great services Columbia offered at its hundreds of hospitals they would bypass competitors' hospitals and go to a Columbia facility. "This is our opportunity to showcase what we already know is good about what we do," Scott had said.

To make the ads memorable, Columbia drew on the expertise of a regional advertising firm, The Martin Agency, out of Richmond, Virginia. Although not that experienced in healthcare, Martin had an impressive client list and some successful campaigns to their credit, including BancOne and Mercedes Benz. Nonetheless, many veteran healthcare marketing professionals were quite surprised at the selection of Martin over larger agencies or those more experienced with healthcare advertising. According to Geoff Crabtree, vice president of strategic planning and market services for the Methodist Healthcare System in San Antonio, Martin presented the best strategic thinking of all the agencies that vied for the lucrative account.

The Martin translation of the Columbia way was to abandon the tried and true approach to hospital advertising, which is either "warm and fuzzy," image-type advertising or service-specific, like promoting cardiac services. Columbia started with a different tack. After conducting focus groups with consumers across the country, the Columbia marketing committee (made up of several hospital marketing professionals from various Columbia hospitals) determined that a nontraditional approach would work best.

Martin executives decided they would have an enthusiastic, self-effacing man off the street serve as the spokesman for the firm. The unassuming healthcare neophyte could "play dumb" about healthcare, while Columbia employees, professional yet empathetic, would enlighten the poor sap. The Martin Agency selected Dan Jenkins, who had just completed a successful stint on Broadway in *Big*, as the endearingly uninformed spokesman. Some speculated that one reason Jenkins was selected was that (aside from his being considerably shorter) he had a rather uncanny resemblance to Rick Scott. However, the fact that he was virtually unknown outside of New York circles, and his ability to effectively play the part, were likely the real reasons he was selected. Like everything Columbia did, the campaign had an ambitious schedule—some speculated, so ambitious that Martin was unable to fully execute the strategic direction that initially differentiated the firm.

The campaign was filmed during the summer of 1996, with a planned introduction to the nation on August 19. In preparation for the national roll-out, there was considerable pre-release hype and internal promotion. Days before the ad campaign hit the print and TV media, each hospital received a "tool box" that included copies of the print ads, videos of the TV ads, and other paraphernalia. The hospital marketing directors were to stage a "special preview" showing the ads to employees on a continuous run video. Columbia employees were given very dark sunglasses (old Hollywood film directors' type) with the Columbia logo displayed prominently on each and a line that read, "Look for me on TV." The idea was that "some day you, a Columbia employee, might just end up in one of the commercials."

The campaign launch was unique, both for its extensive scope and its rapid-fire implementation. Some advertising experts thought the accompanying print campaign was too "busy" (the advertising term for too much copy) and not all that synchronized. One of the print ads, indicative of the overall effort, featured a vaudeville-era sketch of an impeccably dressed, mustached man holding a woman who appeared to have fainted in his arms. The headline on the ad read, "When someone's hurt, nobody ever yells, 'Is there a hospital administrator in the house?'" The body copy then went on to note that few people in distress call for a hospital administrator, but the hospital administrators and everyone at Columbia "are working day in and day out to bring you better medical care."

The "hospital administrator" ad had a short shelf life, not necessarily because it was less than award-winning material, but apparently by design. However, ad critics argued that it was too far afield of traditional hospital advertising, especially for an inaugural piece, and apparently it offended several hospital administrators. These kinds of troubles were symptomatic throughout the print campaign, which some considered too insider-focused and without a consistent theme.

Another ad read, "Hospitals so advanced we're even saving the lives of trees." This ad also had a relatively short shelf life. While no doubt popular among members of the *Sierra Club,* the copy made a rather circuitous attempt at correlating the reduction of paper work with the quality of patient care.

The TV ads performed better. They were hip, disjointed, and comical—everything the Columbia marketing staff wanted them to be. The most memorable ad featured a befuddled Jenkins asking two male farmers standing next to a tractor about services available at Columbia hospitals. The straight line at the close (from Jenkins) was "So, who would you call if you were pregnant in Denver?" to which the older farmer replies, "The six o'clock news." That punch line became somewhat of a rallying cry for the entire campaign. At any number of Columbia presentations, whether delivered by Richardson or Scott, that one-liner was used to spotlight the campaign.

From the start, the branding campaign was controversial. Some industry experts with long memories questioned its viability, because many of the major for-profit hospital chains had tried branding campaigns in the mid-1980s and discovered that they didn't work. So why would this one be different? To these skeptics, Richardson and her staff (with Scott's full support) would respond, "Oh yes, but these times are different and healthcare has changed." Although some skeptics didn't buy it, the rest of the industry followed suit. An article in the September 26, 1996, issue of the *Wall Street Journal* noted that "hospitals are hawking themselves as never before as the maze of healthcare choices makes it tougher to line up patients." The article went on to note that hospital ad spending topped $1 billion for the first time in 1995, up 40 percent from a year earlier. An article in the industry magazine *Modern Healthcare* estimated that Columbia accounted for about 10% of that total ad spending for the industry. As with so many of its initiatives, Columbia galvanized the industry into action. "It's a war," noted Kuyk Logan, vice president for one of Columbia's competitors in Houston, Hermann Hospital, as quoted in the above-mentioned *Journal* article. Even some industry theorists got caught up in the frenzy. Dr. Charles Begley, a University of Texas School of Public Health economist noted in the same article that "hospitals have to advertise. There are just too many empty beds. Right now, it's a consumers' market." The big question remained, "Were the consumers really buying it?" By some measures, apparently so.

After the first wave of advertising, Columbia's market research showed that the campaign had proven effective in elevating Columbia's name awareness. Of course, the more relevant issue—the eventual impact on the business—was not as easily gauged. One argument against hospital advertising is that consumers aren't as involved in the selection process (of healthcare services) as much as with other purchases. For example, the ultimate selection of a hospital is determined by a number of variables, including the patient's health insurance plan, physician recommendation, and the availability of services at the hospital. Selecting a hospital is not like buying a car. Still, as noted by Dr. Begley, Columbia reasoned that consumers were getting more involved in the process, and therefore increased awareness would eventually translate into increased patient volume.

The initial research results indicating increased awareness spurred the group on to even more ambitious endeavors and ideas. Industry articles reported an expected upward spending of $100 million on the campaign. The campaign started up again in the first quarter of 1997 and lasted up until its sudden demise on the day of Scott and Vandewater's departure.

To say that the campaign didn't serve its purpose would be misleading. As noted, the advertising blitz did serve to significantly raise awareness of the Columbia name. Prior to the campaign, less than five percent of the population had heard of Columbia/HCA Healthcare. Precampaign market research revealed that the name *Columbia* was more often associated with movies, sports wear, or the University in New York. (Actually, Columbia University did file a suit to force Columbia to stop its branding efforts in New York, but the court ruled in favor of Columbia/HCA).

In truth, the branding initiative did elevate Columbia's awareness among the public, as intended. In so doing, it arguably achieved a perhaps even more fundamental objective. Given that Scott and his team's key audience was Wall Street, one goal of the campaign (although not often mentioned outside company circles) was to give Columbia's name the prominence and awareness of not just Kellogg's or Campbell's Soup, but of Coca-Cola, Johnson & Johnson, and Federal Express—blue-chip firms that traded at attractive price/earnings multiples, partly because of the name brand awareness and favorable investor perception. After all, if Columbia was to be the Wal-Mart of healthcare, it had to advertise as much as Wal-Mart.

In terms of achieving the fundamental objective of making Columbia a household word, the campaign was an unquestionable success, and Wall Street loved it. Very few if any investment analysts ever bad-mouthed the branding campaign. For the investors (and the analysts that advise them), the branding campaign was a reasonable and effective way to firmly establish Columbia's name and market value in the public's mind. John Runningen, now a healthcare principal with Cordova Capital in Atlanta, but formerly with Robinson-Humphrey, said he thought the campaign was terrific. "Healthcare is becoming more like other industries," Runningen noted. "It's becoming more consumer driven. So the branding campaign made perfect sense."

However, in some respects the branding campaign proved to be a double-edged sword. As with so many initiatives that have affected Columbia's perception and performance, Wall Street's reaction was not as relevant as that of other audiences. For those who opposed the rise and rigors of Columbia/HCA, the branding campaign was just one more confirmation of the firm's arrogance. The nature of the ads—touting its grandiose size, Joint Commission scores, and sheer volume of patients—provided yet another testament to the audacity of the firm and its maverick managers.

Tom Scully, president for the Federation of American Health Systems, said he advised against the campaign. "It was a high-risk strategy" Scully noted in the aftermath of the campaign's analysis. "For those individuals and organizations that didn't like Columbia, it was like putting a bull's-eye on your head."

SALES

Another initiative that Columbia launched to run parallel with the branding campaign was a major effort into sales. While considering Columbia's position among the titans of consumer awareness in the United States, it occurred to upper management that the firm lacked a sales function. They thought if sales worked for Federal Express, Xerox, Johnson & Johnson, and other revered names, why not for Columbia? With that realization, Columbia launched a sales effort to run alongside its marketing campaign. The thought was that where branding would raise awareness, sales would actually bring in the business.

Sales was not a new concept in healthcare. Many hospitals had experimented with physicians' sales representatives of one sort or another in the mid-1980s. These sales professionals, often working under the department of "physicians services" or "physician support" usually worked closely with hospital CEOs in ensuring that doctors were happy with services and in prospecting physicians who referred to competitive hospitals.

Columbia's effort was different; not surprisingly, it was more ambitious. The initiative actually had its beginnings in the Ambulatory Surgery Division (formerly Medical Care America), which already had a rather sophisticated sales effort. Several sales professionals were assigned to territories where ambulatory surgery centers existed. These sales professionals would visit surgeons and referring physicians in an effort to get them to either increase their cases at the surgery centers or start operating at the surgery centers.

Although this concept was sound and seemed to be working, it wasn't enough. Columbia hired a senior sales executive from Johnson & Johnson, Steve Simpson, to develop the internal sales strategy and team. Simpson had worked with physicians throughout his career at Johnson & Johnson, and therefore he knew what doctors wanted and how best to design a sales initiative that would produce meaningful results for Columbia.

One of the innovative components of the Columbia approach to sales was a very focused training for sales professionals. Although this is standard in other consumer or manufacturing industries, healthcare sales training has not caught on with great fervor. As with so many initiatives, however, Columbia was determined to set the standard and position the bar, rather than just raise it a bit. Plus, few if any hospital chains had ever pursued the concept of an extensive sales team, rather than just a sales professional or two.

The sales team's first task was to attend intensive sales training in Nashville, which lasted two weeks. The idea was that eventually all senior executives at each market level would attend a condensed version of the sales training. As Columbia executives put it, "We should have 285,000 sales representatives in this company." This seemed to be a good concept considering the nature of healthcare, which should be the most service-oriented industry in the nation, thus requiring everyone to be a good-will ambassador for the company.

Basically, Columbia was taking the concept of guest relations to a more sophisticated and coordinated level, or at least that was the plan. The idea of guest relations had become popular in hospitals in the mid-1980s with the advent of marketing and increased competition among facilities. However, guest relations (or ambassador training) had never quite received the same kind of attention as afforded in other industries. This was due primarily to a lack of familiarity with the idea, as well as the inability to track results and justify the expense.

Columbia's goal was to change all that. The idea of 285,000 goodwill ambassadors and company sales people was a notion that fired the imagination and certainly intrigued Scott and his senior lieutenants. In fact for all intents and purposes, the sales effort was merely an extension of the contagious enthusiasm that Scott and Vandewater wanted to instill in every Columbia employee. Sales was the formalized vehicle to carry the Columbia message to the masses. No one was surprised then, when Scott announced, "Last month I was focused on branding. This month I'm focused on branding and sales." After all, in most industries the two disciplines complement each other.

Yet for healthcare, the concept of a nation-wide, coordinated sales effort only distinguished Columbia from its competition all the more. Not only was the concept untested, but many strategic questions lingered. Among these was the role of the hospital CEO in the sales process. If a professional sales representative was calling on physicians (a role historically reserved for the hospital CEO), how would that affect the relationship of the medical staff with the CEO? An even more fundamental question raised was, just what exactly does a hospital sales professional sell a physician, and how are the results measured? These were all good questions that arose in the process, but they were without the benefit of precedent in the company or even the industry. The problem was not that the questions didn't have

logical or reasonable answers; it was just that the answers
didn't have empirical results to back them. Columbia was banking on a concept that had worked in other industries with very
different dynamics—something innovators must often do, but
also something skeptics and naysayers would find appalling.
True to form, however, the executives at Columbia paid little
heed to the critics, or even the doubters, and marched ahead
boldly where no healthcare system had gone before.

One area that hospitals and health systems definitely
should have gone before, but few if any had, proved to be an ad-
dendum to the local sales effort, but arguably the most rational
and intriguing element of the sales program. In addition to the
local efforts, Simpson developed a national accounts sales team
that called on the likes of PepsiCo, Wal-Mart, and major suppliers or vendors ("strategic partners" as the company called
them). The notion of national account managers, something borrowed from other industries, was solid in concept and creative in
execution. This initiative was definitely a pioneer effort, as no
other hospital company, large or small, had pursued such an
arrangement at this level.

What made this approach such a sound one was the idea of
staying close to key customers. Most of the healthcare industry,
at least hospital executives and physician leaders, have done a
woefully inadequate job staying close to key customers, namely
large employers. Simpson's idea was both innovative and strategically sound. If Columbia had a dedicated professional that was
in constant contact with a major employer, which had a dual relationship as supplier and purchaser, then the company would
have a vehicle for perpetual market research. Although this idea
did not get the attention some of the other efforts received, it
spotlighted one of the best examples of Columbia's willingness
to pursue the frontier. The sales initiative definitely was on the
vanguard, and like so many Columbia initiatives, it would likely
have been replicated by multiple systems and countless imitators. The viability and value of Columbia's sales initiative will
probably remain untested. With the departure of Scott and
Vandewater, sales lost its chief advocates. Simpson left the firm

in early October 1997 to take a job on the East Coast. Although some divisions and individual hospitals retained the sales function, the effort—orchestrated at the national level—is not likely to ever be replicated.

PRODUCT LINE MANAGEMENT

Another move by the colossal hospital giant was a cross between sales and marketing: the push into product lines. The initiative, which in most industries would have developed out of the marketing department, came under the auspices of sales and Simpson, the sales vice president. In fact, the product line orientation and organization worked in tandem with the sales efforts to promote selected services or areas of excellence within the company's vast portfolio of services.

A few of the initial product lines included oncology, cardiology, emergency services, and behavioral health. Each of the product lines was assigned a national product line manger or director whose responsibility was, among other things, to research his or her particular area of responsibility and determine how Columbia facilities could differentiate their services (for that product line) in each market. Such differentiation could be achieved through clinical research, expanded continuum of services, or merely promoting the level of expertise within the given area.

The concept of product lines was received fairly well and initially did not come under fire. However, in the aftermath of the federal investigations and the blitzkrieg by the press, the media had a heyday with "disease categories as product lines." The notion proved to be (after the fact) one more example of Columbia's business orientation in a traditionally nonbusiness field. In truth, most of the industry probably heard little about the product line initiative until after the investigation had brought that strategy to light in a less than favorable fashion.

Yet Columbia was once again pursuing a strategy that has been tested and proven in many industries, from consumer goods to heavy manufacturing. Procter and Gamble may be the archetypical product management (or brand management as they call it) company, but it is one of a vast host of companies that have found success with the concept. Even hospitals and other components of the healthcare industry experimented with the basics of product or service line management in the mid-1980s. Unfortunately, most attempts failed, given the paucity of experience and the impatience of its architects.

However, for all the grief Columbia has taken for its product line approach (from a cynical press), Columbia may have been slightly ahead of its time, or at least on the cusp of an idea whose time will come. Among the proponents of a service line approach within healthcare are noted authors and academicians, Dr. Stephen Shortell and Dr. Regina Herzlinger. Shortell, who is one of healthcare's best-selling authors and one of its most respected theorists, notes (in his book, *Remaking Healthcare in America*) that in an advanced-stage managed care market, a concept similar to a service line orientation is a viable means to differentiate one's services. Herzlinger, a professor at the Harvard Business School makes a case for "focused factories," in her recent book, *Market Driven Healthcare*. Even though the authors may not agree with the exact notion of what Columbia was pursuing, the idea of segmenting services or categories has merit empirically and theoretically.

Part of the value of isolating particular disease categories or service lines is grounded in clinical and financial structure. As mentioned earlier, the government's push into diagnostic related groupings, or DRGs, created the reimbursement architecture for such an orientation. This was no doubt an integral component of the Columbia model, along with the promotional aspect of the orientation. One area where the clinical component, which had ramifications for reimbursement as well as measurable quality, was with the best practices regimen. An example of this was the emergency services product line. This product line group conducted research and found that one of patients' biggest concerns with emergency rooms (ERs) was the waiting time. The group surveyed some of the best practices data (i.e., best demonstrated practices or best demonstrated processes [BDPs]) and found that a few of the company's ERs were able to see people much faster than the norm. The group, which had the expertise of a former Federal Express executive, Tucker Taylor, concluded that if they could do that at one ER, why not apply the same principles and processes at all ERs within the Columbia network. Characteristic of Columbia's desire to be prominent, as well as pioneering, that concept led to a marketing campaign that touted the improved waiting times of Columbia's emergency rooms.

The thrust of the campaign was that "some emergency rooms at Columbia have been able to improve their waiting times by up to 75 percent." However, the campaign, like other initiatives at Columbia, was more the catalyst for implementation than the conclusion of a successful operational endeavor. As much as any other endeavor, the emergency services campaign, which never took full flight, was indicative of Columbia's drive to get to market with a message, even if it meant the message was substantiated by developing or in-process program operations. The attitude was one that implied, it is "more important that we get the message out first—implementation will follow." Call it the Joe Namath theory of management: Make the prediction and the results will materialize.

With a massive machine like Columbia, that strategy may work once in a while. However, there are only so many times one can preemptively announce an already assumed outcome and get away with it. The sequence of "ready, fire, aim," requires a great deal of damage control after the shooting, as well as an intense amount of prefire effort, since the "aim" component of the equation is delayed. In the final months before the media siege, this strategy was becoming the norm rather than the exception at Columbia, thus exhausting the folks in the field charged with implementation and those responsible for explaining why the promotion seemed inconsistent with perception, or reality.

Nonetheless, this kind of marketing moxie was characteristic Columbia. The firm would rush to market an idea—almost any idea, whether substantive or not. One internal e-mail generated by a Nashville senior staff member captured the appropriate counter response to the emergency room campaign. "If we get 100 percent compliance from *all* the physicians, in *all* the emergency rooms at *all* times, then we can deliver on these outlandish claims."

Such candor was refreshing, but it was also atypical at Columbia. As the company moved toward greater centralization of its operations and its external communications, it became more and more a company that concentrated on conformity and compliance.

A CULTURE OF COMPLIANCE

When Columbia was in its earlier stages, it appeared as though it would be more decentralized and provide more autonomy to local market leaders than its predecessors in the for-profit sector. In fact, this was one of the attractive facets that Columbia offered to prospective partners, as well as executives who considered employment with the company. After all, HCA, which accounted for a large share of Columbia's hospitals, had arguably been the most decentralized of all the for-profit hospital chains. Tommy Frist was an advocate of decentralization, and he was the vice chairman of Columbia. People who had been in the industry a long time knew that HCA had been fairly decentralized, and many assumed Scott would mimic that model. Indeed at first, he did.

One of the Columbia/HCA operating slogans was "centralized accountability with decentralized authority." Columbia/HCA touted its policy of giving considerable financing authority and autonomy to its local mangers—much more so than its predecessors had done, such as AMI or even Humana. Yet as the company started to focus more on operations and less on expansion, the natural tendency toward "centralization creep" began to emerge. (This was confirmed many times after the fact by

Tommy Frist following Scott's departure, when he commented that he was concerned that "the company was moving toward more and more centralization").

Some components of centralization were favorable economically and strategically. For example, one of the elements touted by Columbia executives and competitors alike was Columbia's ability to use its clout to receive "favored nation's" contract prices. Whereas large purchasing organizations like the VHA could not guarantee strict compliance among all its members, Columbia used the methodology perfected by Humana to ensure compliance at its many facilities. In so doing, it could virtually bring millions of dollars of purchasing clout with the stroke of a pen. For the supplier, a Columbia contract meant two things: excruciatingly low discounts coupled with sizeable, guaranteed volume.

One case in point that proved to be a double-edged sword for Columbia was the contract with PepsiCo. According to Columbia executives, both Coca-Cola and Pepsi were approached for major contracts. By entering into an exclusive agreement with PepsiCo, the giant soft-drink company, and promising that Coca-Cola would be the soft-drink non grata (and nonexistent) in all its facilities, Columbia saved millions of dollars—a savings and a strategy that were repeated at multiple Columbia gatherings. On the other hand, the absence of "the real thing" (i.e., Coca Cola) in Columbia facilities proved a sticking point for some employees who saw the move as more of a sign of coerced conformity than a financially sound maneuver. (Translation: Don't mess with people's choice of colas.)

At times the compliance issue was too much to take for Columbia employees, company men and women alike; yet it was definitely part of the Columbia culture. Symbolic of the attitude of the need to "fly the company colors" was the Columbia lapel pin. At first, the pin consisted of the entire word *Columbia*. (At one point, the pin actually read *Columbia/HCA,* but that was so long it was almost like wearing a Tolstoy novel on your suit.) Then the better part of fashion prevailed, and someone suggested that the lapel pin be shortened to the Columbia logo, a large *C*, encased in a baseball diamond–like figure, which purportedly symbolized "healing hands."

The *C* lapel pin was as prevalent at Columbia gatherings as "cheese-head" hats at a Packers game. Pity the poor bounder who was caught without one at a conference or session, especially if a senior executive was there. In fact, Columbia Leadership Conferences had extras at one of the company-sponsored booths. When the booth ran out, forgetful executives had to scramble to find a spare, or risk the intimidating stare of fellow appropriately-bedecked colleagues who had not forgotten the essential item in the Columbia uniform. (Forget your tie or wear brown shoes with a blue suit, but *don't* forget your lapel pin.)

One hospital CEO recounted an incident he had with a senior executive at Columbia who came to tour his hospital. Relatively new to the company, this usually easy-going administrator forgot to wear his lapel pin the day of the tour. Upon meeting the unsuspecting CEO, the Columbia executive sized him up, looked at his vacant lapel slit, and only half-jokingly said, "Next time I see you, I want to see a lapel pin in your suit." So pronounced was the move to conformity that Rick Scott at one point reportedly proposed that Columbia managers wear uniforms. The suggestion was met with such sudden and resounding criticism that the idea was dropped. Nonetheless, the fact that the concept was broached highlights the extent to which Columbia wanted to promote its unique identity and advance the Columbia cause.

Obviously, Columbia isn't the only company that encourages its employees to wear lapel pins or some identifying item. As much as anything, the growing presence of the identity, whether lapel pin, facility signage, or branding campaign to promote the Columbia name, was notice to the world that the company was becoming a fixture in American society and a driving force in the healthcare system. Over 340 hospitals with the Columbia name, a megamillion-dollar advertising effort, a synchronized sales initiative, and nearly 300,000 company ambassadors were all moving in concert to proclaim the merits and market value of Columbia/HCA Healthcare System. Such was the grand vision of Scott, Vandewater, and the firm's powerful strategists. Yet, other powerful groups had a different view of Columbia/HCA and a dramatically different approach to bringing the healthcare colossus into the spotlight.

4

Rough Waters for Columbia

This is as big a case as the government has ever done.
Kirk Nahra, Counsel for the
National Health Care Anti-Fraud Association

THE FBI IN EL PASO

It was not exactly the Ides of March, but for Columbia it was close, literally and figuratively. On March 19, 1997, while Columbia executives throughout the country were winging their way to Washington for their annual meeting, over 100 federal agents, led by the FBI, were serving unsealed search warrants in El Paso. The "raid," as the media chose to call it, was timed perfectly with the departure of not only Columbia's senior management in El Paso, but all of Columbia's senior management.

The El Paso executives first heard about the FBI swarming their facilities in midair, between El Paso and Dallas. As soon as they landed in Dallas, they all changed their travel plans and caught the first plane back home, except for communications assistant vice-president (AVP) Michelle Diaz. She didn't get word about the federal visitors until she was en route to National Airport in Washington. She landed, grabbed her bags, and boarded a plane back to the turmoil in west Texas.

By the time Diaz and the other executives arrived in El Paso, the agents had, for the most part, finished their assignment of carting off files, records, and various documents in "40-foot Ryder trucks." The El Paso executives were able to get back in time to tell the press, "We're cooperating with the authorities at this time. We have not been informed of any of the allegations or scope or nature of the investigation." Perhaps they couldn't comment on the nature, but as for the scope of the investigation, it was one of the largest corporate investigations in U.S. history. The only group seemingly more numerous than the FBI agents were the number of reporters who picked up the story. In newspapers throughout the nation, pictures of dark-suited agents carrying off boxes of records and loading them into the rented Ryder trucks captured the moment with a kind of *Chicago Hope* meets *The Untouchables* look.

Back in the Sheraton Hotel in Washington, D.C., where over two thousand Columbia executives and their spouses were gathered for the annual leadership conference, no one found the pictures or the stories very entertaining. As it played out, the FBI raid seemed not only synchronized (to coincide perfectly with the opening of Columbia leadership conference), but also symbolic. The vast Columbia contingent was meeting in Washington for two reasons. First and foremost, they were in the nation's capitol to celebrate their considerable success and to keep up the momentum. Second, the Columbia entourage had chosen D.C. so they could collectively march on Capitol Hill to inform and impress the "powers that be" within the federal government. Yet on Wednesday, the first scheduled day of the leadership conference, some of the powers that be had provided their own impressive display to Columbia.

If anything can cast a pall over a leadership retreat, it's an FBI raid. Surprisingly, most of the media missed the connection between the Washington leadership conference and the timing of the raid. However, the media did pick up on the symbolism of

El Paso. The fact that the company had started in the sprawling west Texas town just a few years ago, did not escape the attention of the press. Targeting El Paso meant digging at the very roots of Rick Scott's empire. Members of the press speculated that if the investigation started in El Paso, there was no telling where it would lead and when it would stop. For as Scott had often noted, referencing his strategy for building the company, "We're going to do it just like we did in El Paso." What the press wanted to know was just exactly what Columbia had done in El Paso to merit the attention of over 100 FBI agents.

Scott and the management team at Columbia never really answered that question, nor many others that followed in the ensuing days following the FBI visit. Rather, the official word that came from Columbia was similar to the statement out of El Paso, noting that lack of information regarding the allegations limited the company's ability to comment on the scope and nature of the investigation. Rather than spend much time with the press, Scott and his associates remained engaged in the matter at hand—the leadership conference—and communicating to Columbia executives on the subjects they knew best: achieving company growth, keeping investors satisfied, and maintaining the ambitious pace for which Columbia was famous.

The schedule at the conference was indicative of that ambitious pace. As with their other meetings, Columbia executives began the day at 6:00 A.M. with breakfast, followed by the formal program, a speaker or presentation, at 7:00. Usually working through lunch, Columbia conference attendees would conclude the formal proceedings at around 5:30, followed by a postconference reception or recap, allowing a scant 30 minutes or so to prepare for the social event. The evening's festivities would conclude at 11:30 P.M. or midnight, with the next day's agenda starting at the crack of dawn. Such was the storied pace of Columbia gatherings, described by one executive as "the white-collar version of a triathlon."

Such a hectic pace didn't allow much time for reflection, and the Washington conference was no exception. Barely

missing a beat because of the FBI raid, the conference proceeded, with hundreds of executives and guests or spouses
"storming" Capitol Hill on the morning of Thursday, March 20.
Armed with red tote-bags bearing the Columbia logo, a hastily
prepared sheet of issues to discuss, and literature to dissemi-
nate, the group boldly went where no hospital entourage had
gone before and will not likely go again.

Following the morning on Capitol Hill, the Columbia contingent reassembled to hear business luminaries explain how
Columbia could continue to make a difference, in the same way
the speakers' companies had made a difference on the American
business landscape. Most of the program was what one would expect at this type of conference, except for two speakers. In a
solemn session that proved to be unwittingly prescient, conference attendees heard from Harvin C. Moore, director of marketing for Phase One Technology and a former executive in the Texas
savings and loan industry. Moore gave a very dramatic and chill-
ingly effective account of his arrest and subsequent prison experience following a felony conviction for fraud. Little did members
of the audience, who listened with rapt attention, realize how
eerily foreshadowing Moore's speech would prove for a few
of the executives within the audience. However, given the events
that had just occurred in El Paso, many conference attendees
pondered the significance and timing of Moore's presentation.

Another speaker whose timing also proved less than ideal
was Margo Vignola, first vice president and industry analyst for
Merrill Lynch. Vignola, who had covered Columbia for several
years, had likely been given the task of discussing Columbia's
steady stock performance. Ironically, however, her presentation
followed two days of rather severe stock value decline for the
company. Speaking on Friday, May 21, just two days following
the FBI search, Vignola admitted that she was somewhat concerned by the events that preceded her speech. She acknowledged that up to that time, she had been very bullish on
Columbia, but the market's reaction to the FBI news, along with
further speculation on Friday that the investigation could
spread to other cities, left her wondering aloud about the

long-term support of the investment community. (Columbia's stock tumbled an additional six percent on Friday from $41\frac{1}{4}$ to $38\frac{1}{2}$.)

Vignola noted that Columbia shares were something of an enigma. Even though the company continually produced a 20 percent growth in earnings, Wall Street didn't seem to reward the company with the same price-to-earnings ratio of firms that produced similar results, like Johnson & Johnson, which Vignola noted had a similar growth rate. At the same time, the naysayers on Wall Street doubted Columbia's ability to continually produce that kind of growth over the long run. She said that "against the backdrop of a nongrowth industry, aggressive growth posture is a zero sum game." Her key point, which underscored the prevailing negative perception by so many individuals in the country, was that on Wall Street, there is an "ingrained perception that it's not good to make money off the backs of sick people." In essence, Vignola noted that Columbia was caught in a sort of investment catch-22, Wall Street's version of "damned if you do, damned if you don't." According to Vignola, the precipitous fall in the stock's value following the FBI raid was evidence that Columbia's stellar track record for growth was being discounted "because of concerns about public perception, Medicare issues and physician concerns." She noted that investors' reactions to the El Paso events gave some indication of the "fickle, capricious nature of the stock market."

Vignola's candid assessment, highlighted by her professional soul-searching, left the audience with an unusual sense that perhaps the FBI incident was more problematic than it originally appeared. Based on Vignola's analysis, some conference attendees wondered if perhaps Columbia had deeper issues than this isolated event. If support could easily fade, even among its most favored and sought-after audience, Wall Street, maybe the highly-courted allies on "the Street" wouldn't be as faithful as everyone assumed. The truth was, Vignola's speech had such a dampening effect on the mood of the conference, that several attendees were surprised when no one from Columbia followed the analyst to counter with some favorable news or a lighthearted break of some sort. Instead, the conference proceeded on schedule but certainly not as planned.

Nonetheless, Vignola's commentary, coupled with the apparent uneasiness of the group, may have set the stage for what proved to be the defining moment of the leadership conference and a rare glimpse of the rapport Rick Scott had with his company. At the close of Friday's formal program, Scott approached the podium to wrap up the session. Clearly disturbed by media accounts, rising speculation and a host of events swirling out of his control, Scott closed the session with a quote from Abraham Lincoln, given during the height of the Civil War in response to critics who challenged his leadership ability. (Interestingly, Scott cited this same source in his last e-mail just prior to leaving the firm.) As Scott completed the quote with Lincoln's words, "I do the very best I can . . . ," he became visibly emotional, and he left the stage unable to complete his comments. Then in unison, the entire audience of Columbia executives rose to their feet and gave their CEO a 10-minute standing ovation. There followed an occurrence more reminiscent of a rock star's return from his or her last song. Scott bounded back on stage, rejuvenated by the applause of the audience, and enthusiastically encouraged everyone to attend the evening festivities and "have a great time."

It was Rick Scott's last salute and altogether fitting, in a sense. He didn't know it then, but for the entrepreneurial lawyer from Kansas City, who had taken an investment of $250,000 and built a company worth over $20 billion, it was a kind of curtain call. Unbeknownst to Scott and all the people in the Sheraton ballroom, the curtains were starting to be drawn on the colossus Scott had assembled. The vast and impressive empire he had put together was in the throes of a mounting crisis.

REACTION FROM POLITICIANS AND PUNDITS

While the massive Columbia entourage was rallying around Scott and Vandewater in the nation's capital, some D.C. insiders were mounting their own rally. Political figures opposed to

Columbia and the for-profit model of healthcare seized the opportunity to laud the investigation and blast the giant hospital chain. U.S. Representative Fortney "Pete" Stark, easily the most outspoken critic of Columbia within high political circles, immediately went on record to say, "The investigation will spread far beyond El Paso." Meanwhile, two U.S. representatives from the state of Rhode Island, Patrick Kennedy and Robert Wegland, came forward with their views. Each had been actively opposed to the proposed Columbia takeover of Roger Williams Medical Center in Providence, Rhode Island. "Although there have yet to be indictments or arrests, it is safe to conclude that the investigation is very serious," Kennedy wrote in a letter to Rhode Island's Governor Lincoln Almond and reported in *The Providence Journal Bulletin.* Kennedy concluded with, "Particularly alarming to me is that Columbia/HCA is allegedly preying on vulnerable seniors."

Wegland, Kennedy's counterpart in the Second District, went on record in the same article with, "We have heard skepticism about for-profit hospitals since the day Columbia announced its intent to purchase Roger Williams. This investigation in El Paso is just one more red flag raised. Overcharging the government is a serious offense." These were strong words from powerful people. Yet to watch Columbia throughout the ensuing weeks following the El Paso incident, one would not have necessarily assumed that the company was in the throes of a crisis that would eventually alter its entire course and result in a change of leadership.

CALM BEFORE THE STORM

Following the leadership conference in D.C., the pace of market activity increased, but not much was done or said about the incident in El Paso. The number of programs coming out of Nashville multiplied, and the enthusiasm (or zeal, as Scott liked to call it) within the company reached unprecedented levels. As some industry observers noted, that may have been the crux of the problem. Scott and his advisers didn't seem to fully grasp the gravity of the FBI raid. They either didn't recognize or didn't want to recognize that they were in the middle of a bona fide crisis and consequently needed to implement crisis management tactics.

Somewhat ironically, one of the featured speakers at the March leadership conference in Washington was an individual who was familiar with crisis management: Ralph Larsen, chairman and CEO of Johnson & Johnson (J & J). This company perfected the art of crisis management with its astute and now legendary handling of the Tylenol scare. Now, after the fact, Tylenol represents the archetypical template for handling a consumer confidence crisis and is cited by management consultants, public relations professionals, and business school professors throughout the world.

Scott and Larsen had many things in common: Both controlled colossal healthcare organizations, both were tireless workers for their respective companies, and both were creative thinkers not satisfied with yesterday's methods. However, Scott and his team could have taken a lesson from Larsen's firm in how to handle a crisis like the one resulting from the El Paso investigation.

The management of Tylenol readily admitted there was a problem, informed everyone involved of the situation, took immediate corrective action, and focused all efforts on resolving the problem long term. As a result of J & J's astute handling of the crisis, Tylenol, which many pundits thought would end up in the product cemetery with the likes of earlier managerial disasters like the Corvair, emerged in tamper-proof packaging. Eventually, sales of Tylenol exceeded those prior to the crisis.

By contrast, at Columbia there never seemed to be an overt realization of a major problem. The press release from Nashville read simply, "Because the company has not been informed of the allegations underlying the search warrants, the scope and nature of the investigation is unknown." This response did little to assuage concerns or communicate the intent of the company. Yet crisis management is all about response, communication, and doing something, even if it is only the perception that you are doing something to correct the problem.

In retrospect, perception among many key audiences is something Scott and his team never seemed to worry too much about—especially public perception. As Dana McLendon Jr., a former Columbia executive, told *The Tennessean* in mid-July, "When all the facts are known, I believe that any problems Columbia has will not be what they have done, but rather what they are perceived to have done. Sometimes you can be your worst enemy."

STAYING THE COURSE

Columbia executives believed they could ride out the storm of investigations and controversy by rising above it all, keeping their eyes on the prize of growing to be a $100 billion company. For example, Vandewater, the company's COO, had started 1997 by sending out memos to hospital CEOs and division presidents, urging each of them to be "The Renaissance CEO." He encouraged them to provide leadership in their communities through events like Columbia Community Day. He also told them to "take a casual stroll (wear your jeans) through your market's competitor facility. You need to understand their strengths and weaknesses. Do a SWOT (strengths, weaknesses, opportunities, threats) analysis on them. How can you take a value-added approach to outperforming them in your market," he challenged them. This type of competitive spirit was often missing in healthcare. Yet, it permeated the Columbia culture, which cheered executives who excelled to the detriment of their competitors. Although this type of competitiveness is viewed as normal in retailing or banking, it's denigrated in healthcare. Competition may exist, but it must be much more subtle, according to the conventional wisdom in the industry.

Ironically, this memo, written in March, contained some insight into Columbia's coming months. "It's easy to get wrapped up in crisis management in our work," Vandewater wrote. "It's the nature of healthcare that we must devote a lot of resources to treating and managing crises. Just as intensive care is some of the most expensive in the hospital, crisis management is some of the most expensive in the industry. It's costly because it pulls resources from proactive, thoughtful management," he added.

Columbia hospital CEOs, who reported to Vandewater, were constantly challenged to work harder and harder. Some say that too much was expected of them. In a later memo on Renaissance CEOs, Vandewater said this: "It's not enough to be the best planner in healthcare today. Those who are truly effective will be simultaneously skilled at planning *and* selling *and* leadership *and* mentoring *and* be the voice of quality. If you take personal responsibility for running your facility, if you understand the responsibility of your position and use it as a tool to set the agenda for your facility and your employees, and if you keep quality and patient care at the forefront of everything you do, you will help Columbia create the future of healthcare. And you will be a Renaissance CEO."

PRESSURE FROM THE PRESS

In the case of the FBI raid, based on the media's reporting and public perception, the company did not *appear* to be doing much of anything to answer the nagging questions. One mid-May Associated Press (AP) story originating from Nashville had a headline that read, "Columbia CEO Can't Explain Probe." The accompanying article went on to explain how, at the shareholder meeting in mid-May, Scott "didn't answer the question on everyone's mind: why federal regulators are investigating the nation's largest for-profit hospital chain." Scott's position at the shareholder meeting, (which featured heavy security and a Hollywood-style exit by Scott and Vandewater through a side door into two vans full of guards) was disappointingly nebulous for several of the investors in attendance. He said, "As you know, we're involved in an investigation and litigation. We're not in a position to have any public comment." He went on to say that, "Our company is premised on doing the right things. If somebody in the company made a mistake, we'll correct that mistake."

One correction Columbia didn't worry about was the perception that it was moving too fast and aggressively into other markets. While under fire for the government investigation, Scott noted that the government scrutiny wasn't scaring off potential business partners. On the same day he gave his vacuous response regarding the federal investigation, he noted in the same AP article that Columbia was still marching ahead in its plans to take over the University of Oklahoma hospital. "They look at our track record and they're comfortable with our track record as far as I'm concerned," Scott stated. Yet not everyone was comfortable with Columbia's track record.

The uproar at the shareholder meeting was but one example of the growing negative outcry and sentiment toward Columbia. The media didn't help. The *New York Times* ran an extensive article on March 28 that summarized a "year long examination of Columbia." The investigation included a computer analysis of more than 30 million billing records. This extensive review eventually became a backdrop for several other pieces and was reported to trigger a series of investigations into the company's billing practices.

Throughout the spring and summer, the *Times* ran several articles challenging the operations and public perception of Columbia. These investigative pieces written primarily by veteran healthcare reporters Kurt Eichenwald and Martin Gottlieb had a disturbing effect on the company's perception in the circles that read upscale papers like the *Times*. The tone of the articles was captured in a three-page, in-depth piece, again by Gottlieb and Eichenwald, that was the cover story for the Money and Business section of the Sunday edition for May. This piece was titled, "A Hospital Chain's Brass Knuckles, and the Backlash." The article featured a picture of Gray Panther protesters with signs that read, "Stop Columbia," in reference to attempts by Columbia to buy the Roger Williams Medical Center in Rhode Island. Even more damning were accounts of Columbia managers under intense pressure to meet financial goals, nurses who were overwhelmed by increasing patient load because of downsizing, and tales of higher-priced procedures. The article was quite critical, with very little mention of the favorable side of Columbia, other than the fact that Rick Scott didn't cuss, drink, or smoke. Somehow this description seemed to pale against comments by not-for-profit administrators, who in dealing with Columbia noted, "We like to say here that they approached us in a very aggressive manner to marry them. And when we said no, they decided they were going to kill us." This was not exactly the kind of press coverage that finds its way into the annual report. But it wasn't just the *Times* that took shots at Columbia.

The *Wall Street Journal,* the daily forum for advancing the cause of capitalism, did little to advance the favorable perception of Columbia. Perhaps the most damaging article to appear in the *Journal,* prior to the Government's megaraid in July, dealt with a former Columbia/HCA employee named Marc Gardner. The front-page article was titled, "Intensive Care: Ex-Manager Describes the Profit-Driven Life inside Columbia/HCA." In the body of the article Gardner, a 33-year-old former executive who had worked at Columbia's largest hospital in Las Vegas, Columbia Sunrise, noted how he "committed felonies every day." He went on to say that "Columbia hospitals exist to make money—period." He also noted that, in a comparison to one of its predecessor companies, "Columbia was Humana on steroids—20 times more aggressive." The article had few comments from his superiors, among them the sentiment that Gardner had "misrepresented the way we work with physicians and with employees or the way we deliver patient care." However, the *Journal* article did note that Gardner was considering writing a "tell all" book on the subject and was "hoping his story might draw some interest in Hollywood." Gardner was able to draw interest from at least the TV producers. A segment of ABC's *20/20* in August centered around the dramatic claims Gardner had made in the *Journal* article. Although the *20/20* segment noted that he was hoping to get some attention from Hollywood for his story, it failed to mention that Gardner had been counseled by his boss at Sunrise Hospital about his overly aggressive attitude—an attitude he was publicly condemning in Columbia, while hoping to parlay his experience into a Hollywood script. On the *20/20* segment Gardner said Columbia/HCA had been the cause of his becoming "morally bankrupt." He didn't bother to note (as the *Journal* article had) that a few months after his departure from Sunrise he sought employment once again with Columbia in Nashville. When that didn't pan out, he took a job at another Columbia facility in Atlanta.

In a story that wasn't designed to interest Tinseltown, but certainly borrowed a title from a Hollywood film, an industry magazine, *Modern Healthcare* contributed to the criticism of Columbia, with an opinion page commentary (April 14 issue) entitled, "Inside the Predator: Former Columbia executive tells how to avoid becoming the giant's next victim." The self-described former "regional senior vice president" was John Leiffer, who, in the wake of his experience with Columbia, had opened his own consulting firm just to advise hospital executives on how to deal with the "running and gunning entrepreneurial firm." According to Columbia executives in Kansas City, it's doubtful Leiffer ever was an official employee of the firm. Even though he had Columbia business cards printed with his title, he was hired as a consultant to assist with marketing and advertising. Leiffer noted that "Wars are never gentlemanly, and economic conflicts are no exception. I grew tired of the perceived atrocities committed by Columbia." Leiffer elaborated on how Columbia is able to capitalize on weaknesses or vulnerabilities in the market and added that "Columbia is taking no prisoners."

Prisoners, war, and atrocities: These are atypical terms for discussions regarding healthcare. These were also atypical sources for major media stories—a former employee (trying to parlay dramatic claims into a book or movie) and a quasi-employee offering to turn insider knowledge into competitive advantage—both with commercial agendas to advance and alternate career paths to launch. Yet perhaps even more questionable than citing Gardner and Leiffer as "objective" sources was the prevalent use of an early source who emerged in several media reports.

Peter Young, referenced as a "healthcare consultant who's been analyzing Columbia's bills," went on record in national forums, including *The Wall Street Journal, The New York Times, USA Today,* and *NBC Nightly News,* proclaiming the legal and operational irregularities of Columbia. However, an investigative story by the *Nashville Scene* in a September 11, 1997, article titled "Can *The New York Times* Trust This Guy?" revealed that Young had a few irregularities in his own background. The article, written by Willy Stern, noted that "Peter Young is a man with a checkered past. He has been indicted for extortion, and former business partners have accused him of bilking them out of at least $100,000, and perhaps more." Yet none of that information ever made it to the national press. Somewhat inexplicably however, Young's denigrating comments, along with those of Leiffer and Gardner, found a listening ear with highly respected newspapers and news programs—a fact that left some journalism experts wondering, why? Commenting on Young's use as a reference, Dick Schwarzlose, a professor at the Medill School of Journalism at Northwestern, told the *Nashville Scene,* "It's simply not good journalism. The public is entitled to good information and not a bunch of B.S. from a guy who may have a lucrative private agency."

Clearly, the press had it in for Columbia. They didn't always do the reference checks or provide counterbalancing opinions that could have given Columbia executives a chance to challenge or explain the allegations made by its employees and its critics. Part of the explanation for why the media seemed willing to circumvent standard protocol was attributable to the way Columbia handled the press. In the early days of the media blitz following the investigations, there was very little counterresponse from Columbia. For example, in response to *The New York Times* March 29 article on coding and physician syndication, Columbia executives issued the following statement, "Columbia is concerned about a recent *New York Times* article regarding its Medicare coding practices and physician ownership in certain of its hospitals. Columbia was not provided an opportunity to review the *Times* data and was given only a limited description of their methodology. Thus, we cannot specifically address their findings or interpretation." Some people within the company thought such passive and basically noninformative communication was not only inappropriate but implied that the negative information was, for the most part, accurate. Rather than counter the stories, Columbia chose to let the company's activity and actions speak for themselves.

From the media's vantage, the company's actions were speaking for themselves, but not necessarily in a favorable fashion. An article in *The Wall Street Journal* illustrated the dangers with letting the media interpret a company's actions. One thing every healthcare executive learns early and often is never to battle physicians in a public forum because the physicians will almost always win in the court of public opinion. Consequently, the headline in a May *Wall Street Journal* article, "MD vs MBA: Columbia Tells Doctors at a Hospital to End Outside Practice," could not have been worse. The article, written by Monica Langley, detailed an ongoing feud between a Dallas radiologist, Dr. Michael Rogers, and a Columbia administrator, Stephen Bernstein, CEO of Columbia Plaza Medical Center. The story began with Dr. Rogers's recollection of his first encounter with Bernstein: "I was flabbergasted. I thought this is something out of the *Godfather*." That pejorative line pretty much summed up the tone of the article.

The "MD vs MBA" article was significant for two reasons. First, the aforementioned rule of never taking on physicians was seemingly violated by Columbia, in a time when the firm didn't need any more unfavorable publicity. Second, the article produced a flurry of phone calls from physicians, angry at the position Columbia had reportedly taken in Dallas and wondering if that was company policy, an isolated incident, or a misrepresentation by the media. Despite the rationale behind the position Columbia took in regard to the Dallas situation, it left many hospital CEOs and Columbia executives with having to explain their way out of a tough situation.

ZEAL WITHOUT DIRECTION

Even though very little if any formal communication came out of corporate headquarters as a result of the unfavorable articles, there was certainly no shortage of activity in Nashville. The marketing and public relations departments sent out repeated e-mails encouraging hospital staff, board members, and community leaders to write counterbalancing editorials. At the same time, e-mail messages encouraged staff to get out the word on all the good things that Columbia was doing.

Although the intent was good, when a company is facing a media maelstrom, direct and focused communication that responds to the issues is what experts say is best. Columbia never mounted an orchestrated counteroffensive; instead, the focus remained on the branding campaign rather than a coordinated counterbalancing media strategy. The fact that items and issues advanced through the branding campaign were so tangential to questions and concerns raised in the press may have in fact hurt the effort more than helped it. Lindy Richardson, senior vice president of marketing and public relations, would later realize that a more direct approach was essential. She was quoted in a July 13 feature in *The Tennessean* as saying, "We kept thinking our actions would speak for themselves. We were naive, and it didn't work."

At the same time, the executives in charge were difficult to reach and noncommittal when they did respond to the press. Scott and Vandewater scurried about the country, trying to assuage concerns among employees and physicians. They also focused on maintaining good communication with Wall Street analysts. Public perception, as determined by accounts in the media, somehow seemed an afterthought, rather than a priority. One particular incident epitomized the uncoordinated, arguably cavalier, approach to the press. In a speech to the Nashville Health Care Council just weeks after the FBI raid, HCA Vice Chairman Thomas Frist Jr. made comments that an issue of *Modern Healthcare* noted were the "first public comments from Columbia's leadership that didn't come through a prepared statement." In actuality, Frist was subbing for Scott, who had originally agreed to address the group but canceled at the last minute because of a "schedule conflict." The *Modern Healthcare* article went on to note that, "Other than communicating through company spokespeople, Columbia executives have been mum since the March 18 raid."

In a public relations crisis, remaining "mum" is not the recommended strategy. Expectedly, the media immediately picked up on the "no comment" approach, and they milked the situation for everything they could get out of it, with speculation and probing. Some members of the press began to wonder aloud why Columbia was so noncommunicative and evasive. A few reporters even took the Columbia communication's staff to task for their "hostile attitude" toward the press.

Part of the rationale for the nonresponse strategy was self-preservation. Early media accounts following the raid in El Paso were peppered with speculation that Scott himself may have been privy to and approved of sizable and unlawful payments to an El Paso physician, Ambrose Aboud. Aboud had been the focal point of a lawsuit against Columbia by another physician, Lee Schlichtemeier. Schlichtemeier was awarded $6.5 million in damages in March 1997 by a jury that determined that Columbia's business practices had injured his practice. According to an article in the *Dallas Morning News,* Columbia had intervened (financially) between Aboud and Schlichtemeier and caused the disruption and dissolution of a proposed partnership between the two. One particular line of investigation apparently centered around a taped conversation Aboud had with Columbia executives regarding the potential joint venture. The lack of substantive and responsive communication coming out of Columbia's headquarters led one to believe that Scott chose to remain quiet because of his own potential involvement in the investigation and that anything he said in the press or in public "could be held against him." In essence, the Columbia communication strategy seemed to be driven more by legal advisers than professional public relations consultants or media professionals. Soon, even the press began to attack the rather inept handling of the situation. *Modern Healthcare,* which devoted significant space to tracking the Columbia slide, mentioned that Richardson and Scott were nonresponsive to the media. The article went on to note that Scott's vice chairman of the board, Tommy Frist Jr., had been much more approachable by the media. Frist was quoted as saying, "they [the media] always seemed to find me, and I was always willing to talk to them." This merely added to the professional dig Richardson had taken on national TV when Mike Wallace ended the Walt Bogdanich–produced segment on *60 Minutes* with his observation that "Columbia's PR chief" had sent him a fax four days before the show aired. According to Wallace, Richardson wrote, "You've chosen to attack Columbia/HCA rather than provide an 'objective viewpoint.' " Wallace concluded with, "Ms. Richardson we did not attack you. The attorneys general of Michigan and Ohio did." Later he was quoted in *Modern Healthcare* as saying he never encountered such "orchestrated stonewalling."

GROWING CONCERN AMONG THE BOARD

Industry pundits weren't the only ones critical of Columbia's handling of the media, and their hunker down, say nothing to the press mentality. Board members were growing uneasy with the full-steam ahead approach that characterized Scott's response to media criticism and government investigation. Although few members of the media picked up the grumblings, insiders within Nashville and within the investor ranks noted rumblings, especially from Tommy Frist, Jr.

Frist was growing increasingly frustrated at Scott's unwillingness to listen to him or other advisers who advocated an approach contrary to Scott's direction. Rumors began to circulate that Frist had been shut out by Scott and his team. Nashville insiders speculated that Scott's days were numbered, given his falling out with Frist and the mounting negative publicity facing the firm. If Scott had to go head to head with Frist, the makeup of the board favored the HCA founder. Most of the board members were more closely aligned with Frist than with Scott.

Two were former HCA executives (Clayton McWhorter and Donald MacNaughton).

Through it all, it became clear that one of the audiences Rick Scott and David Vandewater appeared to give little time and attention to was their own board. In interviews following Scott's ouster, Frist would note that he had been making suggestions to Scott for months about "easing off" and toning down his aggressive style. These suggestions, according to Frist, went unheeded. Frist's frustration with Scott's failure to respond to his and other board members' suggestions became so intense that he actually considered stepping down from the board around January of 1997.

Whatever negative vibes Scott and his team were getting from the board members, they weren't strong enough to change their course or modify their approach. In fact, in the interim between the FBI investigation in El Paso and the troubles that awaited, the Columbia faithful seemed to intensify their aggressive approach. Each new week brought a program or a project— a new product line or a new community effort. In reality, each week seemed to bring an added "focus," except that of the government investigation. At least, this seemed to be the case until July 16th, when government action precipitated events that were too much for even the "Bill Gates of healthcare" to handle.

G-MEN IN OUR MIDST

July 16, 1997, was a notable day for American industry on two counts. The Dow surpassed 8000 for the first time in history, and it also marked the largest criminal investigative effort of an American healthcare enterprise, that being Columbia/HCA. Over 35 search warrants were served at Columbia facilities in seven states. The July raid dwarfed the El Paso investigation in both scope and media attention. If El Paso was a shot over the port bow, the July effort was more like *The Guns of Navarone*.

The day was marked by media and company frenzy. As word began to spread either via the news or company e-mail that facilities were being served with search warrants, each hospital CEO and senior staff member waited apprehensively for the FBI agents to arrive at the doorstep. Only, it wasn't just the FBI that was involved. This investigation, dubbed "Calling on Columbia" by irreverent industry pundits (after a song that had been written with the same title for the Columbia leadership conference) involved several other branches of the federal government, including the Defense Criminal Investigative Services, the Fraud and Investigative Unit of the Department of Health and Human Services, the U.S. Postal Inspectors Service, and in Utah, the Utah Department of Investigation's medical fraud unit. Kirk Nahra, counsel for the Washington, D.C.–based National Health Care Anti-Fraud Association, told *The Florida Times-Union,* "This is as big a case as the government has ever done."

Most of the facilities involved were in Florida and Tennessee, but facilities in Utah, North Carolina, Texas, and Oklahoma were visited by investigators who removed files, computers, disks, and any relevant information they could find. Other than periodic updates, as to which states were involved in the search, very little communication came out of Nashville, which was described by one company employee as "a command post without a command." Eventually, a press release emerged indicating what the press had already reported, which was that the investigation involved seven states, 35 facilities, and several branches of the federal government. The report also noted that the focus of the investigation was on home care and laboratory billing. This allowed executives at some of the Columbia facilities (those without home care services and/or squeaky clean laboratory billing practices) to breathe a sigh of relief. However, investors weren't among those breathing easily. The news of the extensive investigative efforts sent Columbia's stock plummeting $4\frac{3}{4}$, or a decline of over 12 percent. It was one of the most actively traded stocks on the Big Board, as investors expressed their discomfort with the company's mounting woes. The precipitous fall represented a decline of $3.2 billion in stock market value.

If Scott felt the discomfort, he didn't let it phase his direction or his response. He was scheduled to appear on CNN's *Moneyline* that day. Incredibly, in the midst of the turmoil and despite advice (to the contrary) from his media and investor relations executives, he kept the appointment. He probably should have heeded the counsel of his advisers and taken a rain check. When asked about the investigation (which was the topic of most of the questions) he responded, "It has not been a fun day. But as you know, government investigations are matter-of-fact in healthcare." He went on to note that thousands of hospitals were under such investigation.

Though completely accurate, this somewhat nonchalant statement was the final straw for at least one of Columbia's board members, who told the *Wall Street Journal,* "Rick was saying the same thing he'd been saying for months. At that point, it was clear he wasn't going to change." The board actualized what had been rumored for many weeks within the industry and in Nashville circles: Scott had to be removed from the CEO position, or the attacks and criticism on Columbia would continue to handicap the firm. So began the final campaign to "encourage" Scott and Vandewater to realize that their time had passed. Three days after the seven-state investigation, the board met without Scott and Frist, and Frist, Clayton McWhorter, and Michael Long were given the assignment of breaking the news to Scott. However, in characteristic fashion, Scott maintained that he could hold on.

At this point, according to a September 8, 1997, *Fortune* article (written by Patricia Sellers), Darla Moore entered the picture. Actually, Frist had been maneuvering within the elite circles of the investment world for some time to try to bring the situation to closure. Moore, former Columbia board member and wife of Scott's original partner, Richard Rainwater, had been communicating and collaborating with Frist since the 4th of July weekend. Moore had replaced her husband on the Columbia board in 1994, but she resigned from the board in 1996 because of an investment conflict. Her time spent on the board had given her ample insight into Scott's style, and she had registered (at least in her own mind) concerns about his harried approach and the noninvolvement of the board as related to strategic direction.

Frist had begun soliciting Moore's advice on the situation when he himself felt locked out of the direction of the firm, and with little recourse. According to the *Fortune* article, the final plans were mapped out during that July 4th weekend, when Frist had rearranged his schedule because he felt he had to do something.

Interestingly, Rainwater had continued to advocate for Scott's remaining at the helm, arguing that "Great executives make mistakes, and usually they recover." However, his wife and Frist were unpersuaded, sensing Scott's intransigence, according to an article in *Fortune* magazine. On the morning following the July raid, Scott phoned Moore, who asked, "How're ya doin'?" Scott replied, "Great." Moore reportedly then countered with reality, "Rick, it's over."

In commenting on Moore's role in the ouster of Columbia's founder, Frist told *Fortune,* "Darla was a responsible shareholder who did what had to be done." Yet, what had to be done proved more difficult than originally expected. After having some difficulty scheduling the board meeting to discuss Scott's situation, the board finally convened on Thursday, July 24. With a lengthy meeting expected, the session was started at 4 P.M. Scott did not give in easily. The meeting dragged on into the late evening, with an exasperated and resigned Scott eventually leaving the session to hammer out details of his severance package with his lawyers. (According to a *Wall Street Journal* article written by Lucette Lagnado in late August, Scott originally wanted $30 million but settled for $10 million—$5 million at the time of his resignation and $1 million over five years for "consulting.") The board continued the meeting, eventually adjourning at around midnight.

The next morning the board reconvened. By that time Scott had cleared out his desk and was out of the building and no longer a part of the company he had founded. About 10 A.M. on July 25, the formal announcement came that Rick Scott and David Vandewater had resigned from their positions with

Columbia /HCA Healthcare Corporation and that Dr. Thomas Frist, Jr. would succeed Scott as chairman and CEO of the firm.

Media accounts noted that part of the discussion in the board meeting revolved around a possible merger with Tenet Healthcare Corporation, the nation's second-largest for-profit company. Not only would a Tenet partnership have allowed somewhat of a new beginning for the troubled firm, it would have also allowed for a new leader: Jeffrey Barbakow, the CEO at Tenet. Barbakow was well-known and highly respected on Wall Street for taking the reins at NME when that firm was in the midst of a similar crisis, involving a fraud investigation by the government.

The Tenet possibilities came unraveled for a number of reasons, not the least of which was the difficulty in valuing Columbia without knowing the extent of the fine that would be levied by the federal government if it were found guilty of wrongdoing as a result of the investigation. Interestingly, according to Sellers at *Fortune,* the individual who championed the Tenet arrangement was Moore, who felt that such a partnership would allow Scott to bow out gracefully and still provide the firm with new leadership.

Apparently, bowing out gracefully wasn't in the cards for Scott, the former Wall Street wunderkind who had crafted a colossus out of a nominal investment less than a decade earlier. Scott was left to clear out his desk in the early hours, after failing to win the most important case he had ever argued as a lawyer. Just one year earlier, Rick Scott had been named one of *Time* magazine's 25 most influential people. But on July 25, 1997, he left the company he had founded without even so much as a going away party, leaving behind only speculation on what might have occurred both for Columbia and for the entire healthcare industry—an industry that Scott had successfully challenged and had sought to change.

5

Changing of the Guard

This is healthcare. This isn't GM versus Ford, or Coca-Cola versus Pepsi.

Dr. Thomas Frist Jr.

FRIST AND FOREMOST

Within hours of the board's adjournment, Columbia's new chairman and CEO, Dr. Thomas "Tommy" Frist Jr., started outlining the new direction for Columbia/HCA. The first session involved a conference call with all the senior executives of the company. This was followed by interviews with the press, investors, employees, and several other stakeholder groups. In each of the forums, Frist and other senior executives from Columbia/HCA outlined in broad strokes the new course for the company. They basically established the tone and outlined the strategy of the new regime, while careful not to disparage the achievements of the previous leadership.

Characteristically, Frist diplomatically recognized the efforts of David Vandewater and Rick Scott. Careful not to cast aspersions on their noteworthy efforts, the new chairman noted that it was primarily their style that precipitated the dramatic action of the board. He went on to say, "the issue is what is happening to this company," and commented on what might happen if a change in style and culture didn't come about. He noted that the firm had to gain the trust of the government, something the new management team was 100 percent committed to doing.

In contrast with Scott's seemingly reticent attitude toward the investigation, Frist focused on the gravity of the situation he inherited, emphasizing that the company was in the midst of crisis management and that he and senior executives would try to bring the situation under control.

In almost all of the interviews, speeches, and conference calls, the new CEO made a comment that delineated the dramatic difference between his vision of Columbia/HCA and that of his predecessor. Referencing the initiatives launched by the former management team, including the branding campaign, Frist said, "This is healthcare. This is not GM versus Ford or Coca-Cola versus Pepsi." So much for "healthcare has never worked like this before."

In fact, Frist immediately announced that he would shut down the national advertising campaign and was quite candid about his dislike of the branding concept. Noting that he believed in decentralization, he observed that the company had been moving too much toward centralizing functions and operations. Although noting that some of the initiatives had been favorable, like standardized purchasing contracts, he said, "We have to be careful," in deciding what to decentralize and what to leave at the corporate level.

Frist would often close his comments with the philosophical charge: "It's time for a different style and different leadership. We have to be worried about 1999 or the year 2000—not the next quarter. We need to do what's right."

These central themes would be repeated several times in the ensuing weeks to more groups and media representatives than prior Columbia management had addressed in several months. One thing Frist had maintained (throughout the controversial handling of the media by prior management) was that he always had been and would continue to be more open to the press. He stayed true to his word.

A MORE OPEN POSTURE

Frist and his new team weren't just more open to the press, they were more open, period. Before the announcement of Scott's resignation on Friday, July 25th, the executive area had been under tight security restrictions. Within days of Scott's resignation, the new management team opened up the office area and removed many of the security restrictions—a signal that Columbia/HCA would be more receptive to visitors, employees, and all stakeholders. One Columbia employee commented, "It was like an entirely different atmosphere. With Rick, everything was tight security, limited access. Now, it was like open door policy to the max." Symbolic of the less formal atmosphere, Frist declared the entire month of August as "casual month" for the employees who worked in the Nashville headquarters. As much as anything, Frist was sending a message that the "bunker" approach was over, and it was time to be open not only to the government, but to employees, visitors, the media, and all stakeholder groups.

Nowhere was the willingness to be more open apparent than in Frist's attitude and approach toward working with the government. The new CEO immediately made it clear that he would approach things differently than his predecessor. He intended to develop an action plan and present it to government officials within 10 days, saying, "I have to take decisive action in a responsible way to regain credit and credibility through actions with government bodies." One of Frist's first actions was to engage the Washington law firm of Latham and Watkins to lead the company's examination of Columbia's activities. Commenting on the consolidation of all legal activities under Latham and Watkins's purview, he noted in an interview with AP reporter Kevin Miller, "I'm saying, 'You orchestrate it. You work with us to develop these six, seven things we need to do.'"

He added that, given the work of the legal firm as a backdrop, "We'll go to Justice [Department officials] and say, 'Here's what we're going to do.' and then I'll follow through and make sure they're done." This attitude toward greater openness and a willingness to work with government officials provided stark contrast between Frist's diplomatic style and Scott's approach. Even though both Frist and Scott were pioneers in their own right, they were miles apart in their philosophy regarding healthcare and the appropriate management style.

Frist had spent a lifetime building—not just hospitals, but relationships. He had approached healthcare from the traditional mind-set that physicians were the driving force in the industry on the local as well as national level. Although HCA had been aggressive in its own right, Frist had not announced that he was out to revamp the industry, as much as capitalize on its disorganized and fragmented structure. Frist approached healthcare from a practitioner's perspective. Raised in a family of physicians, he was the insider's insider. He took the traditional model of hospital organization, tweaked it a bit (after the pattern of Holiday Inns, which he readily admitted), and franchised the successful model in multiple markets.

Scott had approached healthcare fundamentally from an outsider's perspective. His initial exposure to healthcare was constructing deals, consolidating systems, and amalgamating assets. At first, Scott seemed more interested in the art of the deal. Unlike Frist, he had not built the system from the ground up; rather, he had reassembled several existing systems into one conglomerate. His belief was that the momentum of the consolidated companies, the accompanying economies of scale, and the sheer size of the assembled megastructure would give him the design (and the clout) to transform the industry.

Whereas Frist's approach was to build, sustain, and expand, Scott's modus operandi was to acquire, amalgamate, and where necessary, consolidate. Scott did not appear to be particularly interested in relationships outside his own circle of influence. From the outset, he had cast Columbia as a kind of market maverick—neither friend nor collaborator within the industry. In Scott's opinion, the not-for-profit model was out-dated and ill-suited to meet the dynamic changes of the health-care market. Not-for-profit hospitals, in essence, represented an anachronism, whose very tax-exempt status he challenged as sub-optimal. Claiming that for-profit hospitals actually provided more community benefit than their not-for-profit counterparts, he verbally attacked the vast majority of hospitals within an in-dustry in which he was a relative newcomer.

Consequently, when Frist assumed his role as CEO of Columbia/HCA, part of his task was to reconstruct bridges his predecessor had burned. As he later noted, "We are presumptu-ous and arrogant if we think we can set the standard for an in-dustry that is 80 percent not-for-profit."

Scott had assembled a cadre of senior executives who fol-lowed his lead and shared his vision. Understandably, when Frist replaced Scott at the helm, his game plan called for a team that shared the new vision and the new style. Vic Campbell, se-nior vice president of investor relations, summed it up in a statement in *The Wall Street Journal* soon after the change in leadership: "We have a new coach and a new game plan, which ultimately leads to new players."

CHANGES AT THE TOP

Frist wasted no time in reconstructing his management team. Within one week of his assumption of responsibilities, he hired Jack Bovender as president. Bovender was no stranger to HCA or to Frist, having served as chief operating officer until 1994, at which point he had chosen to resign when the merger with Columbia was completed.

Bovender was known as a hardworking, no-nonsense kind of leader. He wasted no time in making his philosophy known through interviews with the media. In the August 11 issue of *AHA News,* Bovender made his approach to business clear: "The ethical practice of business is absolutely essential. It not only makes sense from a professional standpoint, but it makes good business sense over the long haul, because nobody wants to do business with someone they don't trust."

Following Frist's lead, Bovender also wasted no time in clarifying Columbia's new approach and role in the industry. Three days after he joined the Columbia/HCA team, Bovender and Frist announced sweeping changes in the companies operations, which included the 12-point plan, as they termed it. Among the changes they proposed were the following:

- Elimination of annual cash incentive compensation for senior and middle management
- Sale of the home-care division
- Discontinued sale of physician interests in hospital and unwinding of existing physician ownership interests
- Adoption of a comprehensive compliance program
- Increased disclosure of Medicare cost reports
- Change in laboratory billing procedures
- Increased review of Medicare coding practices
- Stronger guidelines for all transactions with physicians

A few of these practices had been controversial from the outset; therefore the move to divest or discontinue some of these initiatives was greeted with mixed reviews. However, many industry experts and outside observers felt the decisive action represented a sound strategy and a move that may have been necessary, given the spate of bad publicity leading up to the change in management.

UNWINDING CONTROVERSIAL PRACTICES

One of the most controversial initiatives Columbia had promoted was its physician syndication. As described earlier, the concept had been tried at several for-profit hospital chains. Scott had caught onto the idea after he was involved in the Republic arrangement. Republic executives were some of the most ardent advocates of physician ownership. Physician syndication allowed physicians to invest financially in the overall performance of their individual markets. During Columbia's early years, syndication had been attractive and lucrative for many of the participating physicians. It had also been a lightning rod.

Representative Pete Stark, a Democrat from California, had been vehemently opposed to the physician ownership model of Columbia, citing what he believed was an inherent conflict of interest. Stark had proposed legislation that related to physician-owned laboratories and had advanced similar legislation for hospitals. Although the latter had never been tested in the courts, physician ownership had few defenders within the industry (outside Columbia circles) and many opponents, as Stark was not alone in his opposition.

Many physicians and hospital administrators felt that even if the practice was technically legal, it violated ethical principles, giving physicians an economic incentive to refer paying patients to Columbia hospitals while sending nonpaying or heavily discounted patients to other hospitals. Physician ownership also put not-for-profit hospitals at a competitive disadvantage, as they could not offer such financial arrangements to referring and staff physicians.

The variable perhaps most important at this point in time was the fact that Tommy Frist said he had never liked the concept. In a speech to an institutional investors group in late September of 1997, Frist noted that when HCA had purchased General Care in 1981, the eleven hospitals involved each had about 50 percent physician ownership. Because of Frist's uneasiness with physician ownership, HCA had eventually unwound the ownership practice in nine of those hospitals and sold the remaining two hospitals. Commenting on physician relationships, Frist told *Modern Healthcare* reporter Bruce Japsen, "There's no practical reason to do them. Physicians want a place that has atmosphere and warmth and a place where the patients are happy and the employees are happy."

Consequently, one of Frist's first official acts was to immediately stop the practice of physician syndication with a promise to eventually unwind all such arrangements. This action was an important symbolic gesture and provided an immediate peace offering to the government. The cessation of the branding campaign had meant little to the government, although it was undoubtedly a reminder of Columbia's unwavering zeal. Branding was more of a nuisance than an obstruction of justice. However, from a perceptual standpoint, physician ownership was far more controversial because it could be viewed as providing an opportunity for "crossing the line," as Stark had said.

A similar potential for crossing the line was also the rationale for dismantling the incentive bonus program for Columbia management. Under this program (which involved thousands of Columbia/HCA managers, from hospital directors on up), Columbia employees could receive a significant bonus for their success. Bonuses ranged from 5 to 10 percent of base pay for department directors and much loftier percentages as rank and responsibility increased. Incentive bonuses were based primarily on achieving predetermined financial targets, with some variability for patient satisfaction and quality measures. Clearly, the major determinant of bonus eligibility was financial and heavily dependent on the individual facility.

However, unlike physician syndication, incentive pay (for financial performance and other operational indicators) is quite common within the industry. Not-for-profit hospitals, as well as for-profit facilities and systems, are known to provide incentives for performance to their middle managers and senior executives. Columbia's program may have been more extensive in its breadth and visibility, but the concept is pervasive throughout the industry. What may have differentiated Columbia's programs from other hospitals was the ambitious basis on which the financial targets were established. As mentioned earlier, Columbia had annual corporate earnings goals of 15 percent or better. These often translated into 20, 30, or even 40 percent increased earnings targets for individual hospitals or market divisions. In the early years, while the company was in its rapid-fire acquisition mode, such targets could be achieved. However, as acquisition possibilities began to diminish, and ability to capture market share from competitive hospitals became more difficult, the targets became more challenging. CEOs in some markets saw the goals as unrealistic in an industry where admissions were essentially flat.

Word of the unrealistically ambitious targets ("stretch goals," as Scott and Vandewater called them) began to surface within the industry and the media. Disgruntled employees complained to reporters and to industry colleagues, who notified the press. They also complained to Frist.

By the time Scott resigned, it was widely known throughout the industry (as well as the media that reported on healthcare) that Columbia had atypically high financial targets for their executives and that a significant component of their compensation depended on hitting those targets. Consequently, some industry observers concluded that if Columbia employees were operating in the gray area, it could well be the fault of the cash carrots dangled before them via the bonus incentive program. Frist wasted no time getting rid of the program. In an August 7 Columbia/HCA press release, Frist noted, "This change puts the emphasis in our compensation structure where it should be, on providing long-term focused compensation . . ." Addressing the potential for perceived conflict, Frist further stated, "Eliminating short-term cash incentive compensation will simply remove any appearance of pay being tied to short-term objectives."

Still, the largest potential for abusing the system was home care. Early reports from the FBI raids had indicated that the investigation centered around two areas, laboratory billing and home care. In its rapid growth spurt, Columbia had created the largest home-care operation in the nation, with over 590 home-care locations spread across 30 states. In response to the pending investigation, Frist offered to sell the entire home-care division. Rather than wait until the government cited the company for problems, Frist offered to divest before he was ordered to divest. In the same press release that discussed cash incentives, the sale of the home-care division was mentioned, noting that, "While Columbia will continue to provide a broad range of comprehensive services, the company plans to divest its home care division."

These initiatives—physician syndication, incentive bonus program, and home care—were all offered to the Justice Department as good-faith efforts that Columbia would do whatever it took to resolve the investigation and proceed with its core business of treating patients. There were just two problems that arose. The desire for expediency in cooperating with the government, coupled with loose lips, meant that most employees found out about the plans by reading the newspaper, rather than reading about it on e-mail or hearing it from their supervisor. On Wednesday, August 6, 1997, the *New York Times* ran a detailed article citing the report Columbia had presented to the Justice Department the previous day. Someone at the *Times* had been given a leaked document of the Justice Department proposal. By 8 A.M. the majority of Columbia employees had read about the proposals in their local papers, many of which had picked up the story from the AP wire. So home health employees across the country found out their jobs were at stake by reading the business section of their local paper. Thousands of middle managers and senior executives found out about the plan to cease the incentive bonus and that the program had been dismantled.

The other problem with these dramatic changes was that not everybody at Columbia agreed with them. The plan marked a radical departure from the Rick Scott and David Vandewater approach. It was more than a question of style; it was a basic issue of healthcare management.

Some of the senior executives in the company were very much aligned with the concept of physician investment. After all, weren't physicians their partners? If the option for financial investment by physicians were removed, how much of a true partnership could occur? Additionally, physician syndication offered a clear competitive advantage, especially against the not-for-profit hospitals. Not-for-profit hospitals were legally prohibited from selling a piece of the action to doctors, although hundreds have "for-profit" joint ventures in outpatient businesses.

Scott's approach hinged on the belief that the way to achieve success was through financial means—for physicians, employees, managed care organizations, and employers. Frist's style hearkened back to a more traditional model, where relationships and quality service are just as important, if not more so than monetary considerations.

More controversial than the physician issue, which had relatively few champions, was the issue of home care. Although the home-care division represented only about five percent (roughly $1 billion) of Columbia's near $20 billion revenue, it was a critical component of Columbia's integration strategy. Without home care, Columbia would lose a valuable link to posthospital treatment, and its continuum of care would be interrupted. "Home healthcare has helped growth of a number of their hospitals, not just their underperforming ones," noted Peter Costa, healthcare analyst at ABN AMRO Chicago Corporation, in a *Reuters* article. Nonetheless, Frist and his team maintained that home-care services could be connected via strategic partnerships. "You don't have to own all components of the delivery system," he noted on a conference call. Yet many managers and strategists within the ranks of the company felt that divesting home care was not only unnecessary but could prove unwise, from a strategy standpoint.

Despite the internal concerns over divesting home health, the preemptive move to divest that component of the company's business may have avoided some difficulties. An article in *The Wall Street Journal* described the government's investigation into documents, indicating that Columbia realized a profit of between $6 and $15 for each Medicare patient visit. This finding was problematic since home-care companies are cost reimbursed and "aren't allowed to profit from Medicare and Medicaid beyond reasonable salaries and expenses for operation and employees." The "profit" was generated from allegedly shifting the costs for operating the hospital onto the home healthcare business.

The *Journal* article drew from Columbia documents that spelled out earning targets of $188 million on revenues of $1.3 billion and suggested that the home-care division "was dollar driven instead of driven by patient need." Another revealing article in the *New York Times* detailed the role of subsidiary cost reports in billing Medicare for home-care visits. That article noted that "Columbia employees have told investigators they were instructed to keep these documents secret and to not show them to Medicare auditors."

In truth, Columbia's problems with home care were not unique. Of all facets of healthcare, home care presents the greatest opportunity for fraud. In fact, several cases outside of Columbia's operations highlighted bogus home-care operators, for example, owners adding in the overhead of their son's BMW as an operating expense, entertainment trips to the Super Bowl, and even billing for nonexistent patients. Columbia managers noted that even though home care may be getting a bad rap on the whole, Columbia's operation was sound financially and legally. Perhaps this was true, but Frist and his team felt the implication by association was too great to run the risk of retaining the home-care division.

Nonetheless, it was a risk, along with the other changes, that Frist was willing to take. Frist told Kurt Eichenwald in an interview with the *New York Times* in late August that, "I finally realized that if things didn't change, that it would all come down under its own weight. The government actually did us a favor because it let us address an underlying issue and that was the way you go about running this company."

The speed and thoroughness of these proposed changes proved too much for many Columbia executives. In the next few months, 11 of the top 14 Columbia executives would resign, including the company's CFO, who started working the week Scott was ousted. The same week the proposal was leaked to the *New York Times,* the senior vice president of strategic development, Dr. Herbert Wong, resigned. Wong was a seasoned executive who had worked for AMI in the late 1980s and was an early pioneer in patient satisfaction studies. Wong had been instrumental in developing the concept of disease management, product line development, and Pacific Rim expansion. Many of the research and development efforts that were beginning to take shape were attributed to his creativity and willingness to consider and develop strategic initiatives that were both innovative and potentially symbiotic.

Shortly after Wong resigned, Jamie Hopping, president of the Western Group and a former Florida region CEO, announced that she was leaving the organization. Hopping was responsible for all the hospitals west of the Mississippi. She was replaced by Richard Bracken, who had left the company earlier. The resignations, or "mutually agreed upon" career decisions, continued in the ensuing weeks. Senior management positions weren't the only elements discontinued at Columbia/HCA. The dramatic change in direction also resulted in several projects and pending deals being abandoned.

DEALS SCUTTLED, DEALS LOST

Much of the slowdown in Columbia's activity was voluntary, whereas some of the pending arrangements were abandoned by other parties. One example was the controversial Roger Williams Medical Center in Providence, Rhode Island. In late August Columbia broke off the arrangement with executives at Roger Williams, with its CEO telling *Modern Healthcare,* "We will respond to approaches that have been made to us in recent weeks and we will reach out proactively to other potential partners."

In that same week Columbia announced that it would withdraw as a contender for a contract to manage the University of California Irvine Medical Center in Orange, California. Senior Vice President Vic Campbell commented on the situation, telling the press, "We're looking internally right now. We're moving out of an acquisition phase into an operational phase." Commenting in *Modern Healthcare* on the withdrawal, the executive director of the hospital stated, "With all its recent activities, Columbia has decided to focus its attention on other pressing issues with the organization."

One of those pressing issues included the divestiture, or at least partial (three-fourths) divestiture of a company that had just been purchased by Columbia three weeks previously—Value Health Inc. The Value Health acquisition had been in the works

for several months, but it had been delayed pending approval
from the State of California. No sooner was the approval obtained
and the announcement made, when Columbia announced its
intention to sell three of the four components of the $1.1 billion
company. Regarding the rapid turnabout, Frist stated in a
Columbia/HCA press release, "The decision to pursue divestiture
of these subsidiaries is part of our strategy to refocus our basic
business of delivering quality healthcare services to the more
than 100,000 patients we serve each day in our local hospitals."

THE DAILY COLUMBIAN

Despite the dramatic changes proposed by Columbia, the investigative forces, with the media always on their heels, kept
up the pressure. The *New York Times* may have "scooped" the
story on the report to the Justice Department, but for sheer
volume, the ensuing weeks belonged to *The Wall Street
Journal*. Each day, on pages A2 or A3, the *Journal* featured a
juicy story on Columbia. First came the revelation that
Columbia itself was the target of the criminal probe, not just
individuals within the company. Few firms have been the target of such a criminal indictment, and none were in the healthcare industry. Next came the news that Columbia employees
may have destroyed documents related to the investigation. An
unnamed citizen had reported that a trash bin, miles from El
Paso, had been the repository of mounds of Columbia documents. Following this news came word that the controller for
the largest pension fund in New York, Carl McCall, was suing
Columbia's director and senior management for "gross mismanagement" of the company's assets. Then on Friday, August
15, the *Journal* reported that HealthSouth, the nation's largest
rehabilitation company, had made an unanswered bid for
Columbia—either in its entirety or in parts. The final announcement gave the stock an upward tick, which was a
blessed relief for investors who had seen it fall several points
with each new revelation.

SUITS, SUITS, AND MORE SUITS

As if the press and the investigation weren't enough, the dog days of August brought another distraction: shareholder lawsuits. Although the March El Paso raid had precipitated a few minor suits, the catalysts for shareholder activity didn't occur until mid-August. As noted earlier, H. Carl McCall, New York State Comptroller, filed suit on behalf of the New York State public pension funds. McCall brought the suit against 11 current and former executives and directors of Columbia/HCA, citing that the individual had allowed "pervasive and systemic" criminal fraud to flourish throughout the company. Elaborating on his position, McCall was quoted in the *New York Times* as saying, "Their reckless mismanagement and abuse of control by certain officials with Columbia/HCA has resulted in one of the most extensive and widespread Federal fraud investigations in history. The company and its shareholders should not have to pay the price for the fraudulent actions of these individuals."

One price that investors were having to pay (at that time) was an approximate 30 percent decline in the stock value since the El Paso investigation had been launched. The stock price had been trading at around $44 per share prior to the El Paso raid, but it was hovering in the low thirties at the time McCall filed his suit.

McCall's action opened the floodgates for other major pension fund managers and executives. Within a few days, two other large public pension funds filed shareholder lawsuits. The Florida State Board of Administration and the Louisiana Teachers Retirement System both filed suits, seeking damages from Columbia directors and executives. Tom Herndon, executive director of Florida's State Board of Administration, acknowledged the moves by Frist to change the company's course; however, he told the *Wall Street Journal*, "They are taking positive steps, but they don't necessarily eliminate the cloud hanging over the company's head." In a statement of paradoxical reasoning, Walton Bader, a New York attorney who filed the suit in behalf of both large pension funds, cited several controversial business practices that led to devalued stock. Among these practices was "Columbia's primary goal of turning a profit, which has led some critics to accuse the hospital of giving poor treatment to patients who couldn't pay, hiking up what it charges the patient for single items and skimping on care to save money." He further noted, "We felt that's been very bad for the image of the company and some people wouldn't want to invest in Columbia because of that," as quoted in the *Tampa Tribune*.

Whether the company had done all those things in its goal to turn a profit was an ongoing debate, but as Hendon had said, the storm clouds continued to gather as media reports revealed that more than a dozen federal whistle-blower suits had been secretly filed against the beleaguered hospital chain. A report in the *New York Times* mentioned that many of the individuals who filed suits had provided information to the government that was used in developing the criminal inquiry. News of the whistle-blower suits was especially disconcerting because it signified that federal officials had an inside line to the company's operations some time before the inquiry was launched. As Columbia's Vic Campbell told the media, "We are interested in seeing any accusation. The sooner we see them, the sooner we can respond to them."

Compounding the company's problem even more, private insurers began their own investigation into Columbia's billing practices. Allison Duncan, a partner with the Washington law firm of Wiley, Rein, and Fielding, was retained to represent several large insurers in evaluating whether the healthcare colossus overbilled the insurers.

LEGAL PROBLEMS DOG COLUMBIA

More disconcerting than the lawsuits was the ongoing criminal inquiry. Less than a week following Scott and Vandewater's ouster by the board, three senior executives were indicted on chargers of intent to defraud the government. The three indicted were Jay Jarrell, Michael Neeb, and Robert Whiteside, all of whom had worked at Columbia Fawcett Memorial in Port

Charlotte, Florida, in the late 1980s. Interestingly, the scope of the indictments began prior to Columbia's owning the hospital. Fawcett had originally been owned by Basic American Medical, an Indianapolis firm acquired by Columbia in 1992. However, Whiteside, at the time of his indictment, was serving as Columbia's reimbursement director in Nashville. Jarrell and Neeb had long since moved on to executive roles in other areas of the Florida operation. Commenting on the indictments, U.S. Attorney Charles Wilson stated, "This indictment . . . represents the first phase of the government's ongoing investigation of Columbia."

On the same day the indictments were announced, Columbia reported its earnings for the second quarter of 1997. On CNBC, Sheryl Skolnick, a senior analyst at Roberston Stephens, outlined Columbia's impressive accomplishments, noting that the firm had reported a 15 percent increase in second-quarter profits. Unfortunately, Wall Street greeted the news less than enthusiastically because of the indictments and a concern as to when the other shoe would drop and more such action would be announced.

They didn't have to wait long. The day following the first three indictments, federal officials announced that "dozens" of Columbia/HCA officials could be indicted, and they were likely to be additional employees at Columbia's Florida operations. Even more distressing to investors (and Columbia executives trying to resolve the issue) was the expected length of time to complete the investigation. "As you're aware, we executed a lot of search warrants," noted Albert Robison in the *Tampa Tribune,* who was the special agent in charge of the FBI office in Tampa, Florida. "It's going to be a lengthy investigation and we just have to be patient." Quantifying that, Ben St. John, a spokesman for the Inspector General's Office in the U.S. Department of Health and Human Services, stated that "the probe could last more than three years."

Many people inside and outside the industry have commented on Frist's handling of the government investigation. Some have felt that he offered up too much before a decision from the government. Others have felt that he needed to demonstrate a sincere desire to work with the federal agents, given the approach of prior management.

In the forum for investors in September, Frist gave some insight into his approach when he cited a precedent from the investment banking industry. He noted that in the 1980s two major firms had come under federal investigation: Drexel Burnham Lambert and Salomon Brothers. Drexel Burnham had chosen to fight the government and to "deny, deny, deny." On the other hand, Salomon Brothers had cooperated fully with the federal investigation. As Frist noted, only one of those firms is around today, that being Salomon Brothers.

Apparently Frist and his advisers felt that the investigation was serious enough to merit dramatic measures. The other strategy was just too much to risk, given the potential outcome. In fact, in a move that marked a first for the healthcare industry, in mid-October Frist announced the appointment of Alan Yuspeh as Senior Vice-president of ethics. Yuspeh had gained national notoriety as the key individual responsible for orchestrating an ethics and compliance program for the defense industry in the 1980s.

On the heels of that appointment (in early November) and as part of his 100-day plan, Frist appointed Dr. Frank Houser as medical director and SVP of quality. He also named Robert Waterman as Columbia/HCA's general counsel. At the same time, he and Jack Bovender unveiled a mission and values statement designed to "put the patient first."

6
CHAPTER

Other For-Profit Firms

I'm sick about it. Some people watch *60 Minutes* and they tend to lump us all together.

Alan Miller, chairman and CEO of Universal Health Systems

Although Columbia received most of the attention and criticism as it hit overdrive in the 1990s, other investor-owned hospital chains were building their systems as well. Many flew below the radar, and few were as aggressive as Columbia.

TENET HEALTHCARE CORPORATION

During the weeks that management turmoil reigned at Columbia in July 1997, word of a possible merger with Tenet surfaced. Executives from both sides remained silent, refusing to elaborate beyond a *Wall Street Journal* story that was based on more than mere speculation.

Ironically, it was Tenet's own tumbles with the law that gave merger talk credibility. Formerly known as National Medical Enterprises (NME), Tenet spent the early 1990s in a kind of corporate dialysis, purging impurities from its own bloodstream. With the acquisition of American Medical International (AMI) in 1995, Tenet appeared ready to shed its past and go forth anew: an 84-hospital chain with $5 billion in annual revenues.

Tenet resulted from the March 1995 merger of NME and AMI. The company had very different histories although both had roots in southern California. Tenet remains based in Santa Barbara, California with its operations center in Dallas, Texas (AMI's former home).

Since 1991, AMI had been led by Robert O'Leary, who had no experience with for-profit chains until he was hired by AMI's board in 1991. O'Leary's roots were in the not-for-profit hospital sector, and to that sector he returned after a spin in the driver's seat at AMI. O'Leary now leads Premier, the nation's largest group-purchasing alliance for not-for-profit hospitals.

Today Tenet is led by Jeffrey Barbakow, a former Wall Street banker who knew much about finance but little about healthcare before leading the nation's second largest hospital company. However, since being named to the chain's board in 1993, Barbakow transformed the company's financial and organizational structure while somehow managing to retain the laid-back composure that becomes southern Californians. Unlike Scott, he doesn't profess to change the industry. He focuses on Tenet alone and sees himself as its chief strategist. "I try to figure out where all this is going," he emphasized in an interview in 1995. (Given the various subdivisions and reconfigurations, it's easy to understand why. Figure 6–1 on the following page depicts the "evolution" of the two largest systems, Columbia and Tenet.)

Barbakow (a 50-year-old father of two sons) began his financial career at Merrill Lynch in 1969. There he focused on healthcare, media, and entertainment industries, managing debt and equity financings and leveraged buyouts (LBOs). He was managing director of Merrill Lynch's Los Angeles office when Metro-Goldwyn-Mayer/United Artists Communications (MGM/UAC) tapped him to reposition that company. After boosting MGM/UAC's cash flow and stock price, he engineered

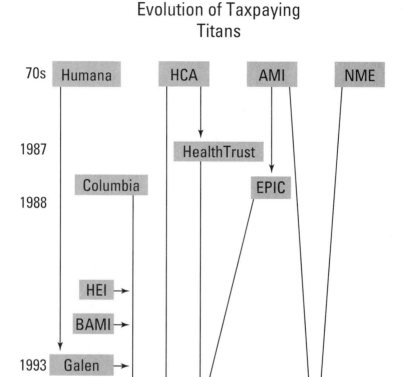

Evolution of Taxpaying Titans

Figure 6–1

the company's sale in 1991 to Pathe Entertainment Group. Barbakow then became managing director of Donaldson, Lufkin & Jenrette, a Wall Street investment banking firm that would later see Barbakow as one of its best customers.

Two years later he took over the top slot at the struggling NME. (Interestingly, Tenet headquarters were just across the street from MGM in Santa Monica until recently.) His job at NME, which is now called Tenet, was straightforward. Some industry observers argued that the company had nowhere to go but up; in other words, you can't fall off the floor. However, it could have been worse. Barbakow himself would acknowledge that NME might have been forced into Chapter 11 bankruptcy in late 1993 or early 1994 by its banks if he had not been able to pull the right financial strings.

In the final negotiations to buy AMI, NME decided to wipe the slate clean and change its name to symbolize its new direction. The name Tenet was chosen form some 1,600 possibilities and carries the connotations of high ethical standards and principles. The name is particularly relevant since NME was tarnished in the early 1990s by its own fraud investigations, lawsuits, and financial losses stemming from its 65 psychiatric hospitals.

Psychiatric care was the downfall of NME's three founders, all of whom resigned in the wake of allegations that their psychiatric hospitals defrauded patients, insurance companies, and the government. As noted earlier, NME's founder John Bedrosian was on a growth mission in the 1980s. To an acute-care hospital chain like NME, psychiatric care was an overripe tomato just waiting to be picked from the vine. This is because psychiatric hospitals were less expensive to build and cheaper to staff than acute-care facilities, which takes care of the cost side. Regarding the revenue side, payment was based on charges rather than fixed-price diagnosis-related groups (DRGs). As in the early days of Medicare, providers could charge whatever the market would bear, and insurance companies would pay it. There was little accountability, as the insurers soon found out. Eventually, they sued, charging NME with fraudulent billing practices.

Yet, it all sounded very believable at the time. In the late 1980s, some providers were backing up their huge expansion plans with statistics suggesting that one in five Americans had some psychiatric problem and that one in three had an addiction. Even if such statistics were true (which is questionable) it's doubtful that all of those patients needed to be hospitalized. Still, the newly built psychiatric hospitals couldn't turn a profit unless they were filled with patients, and this translated into a somewhat twisted glee on the part of psychiatric managers and employees at finding individuals with mental health problems. However, by the early 1990s, everyone—insurers, government officials, consumers, and especially lawyers—was on NME's case.

The day that will go down in infamy for NME employees is Aug. 26, 1993, when hundreds of federal agents surprised NME officials and seized patient records from the headquarters and regional offices. From that point on, much of the company's agenda was determined by the legal ramifications of that wide-ranging federal investigation.

In 1994, NME signed a $379 million settlement with the federal government over alleged fraud in its psychiatric operations. As part of the settlement, the company also was ordered to divest its psychiatric hospitals and institute a company-wide ethics program that continues to this day. It was that ethics program, which includes a toll-free hotline for employees, that was hailed as a model in the wake of Columbia's problems. Tenet was held up as a shining example as critics noted Columbia's lack of such a program.

Tenet grew in size again in 1997 when it purchased OrNda Health Corporation, a Nashville-based chain that had emerged from the ashes of Republic Health Corporation. Republic was a Dallas company that went through an ill-fated LBO in 1986. The company recapitalized, restructured, reorganized under Chapter 11, and emerged, seemingly revitalized, for the 1990s. OrNda's new start came under the watch of Charles Martin, whose roots in this industry trace back to the 1960s and General Care Corporation. Martin rose through the HCA ranks and was one of three key managers chosen to lead the spin-off of Healthtrust in 1987. Revered for his quick financial mind, yet regarded by some as temperamental, Martin was COO of Healthtrust. Under Martin's tutelage, operating margins at Healthtrust increased from less than 14 percent to 18 percent within two years. They continued to improve to over 20 percent within four years.

Then in September of 1991, Martin left Healthtrust. His four-year stock options had vested, and he was ready to move on. "I was interested in getting where I had a bigger fraction of the action," Martin quipped. He formed his own firm, the Martin

Companies, and signed a letter of intent to buy seven hospitals from Safecare. He was in the middle of completing that deal when he got a call from one of Republic's venture capital backers, Paul Levy, who asked if Martin would consider running Republic.

Martin said yes, and by January 1992, the 49-year-old industry veteran was back in the saddle as chairman, president, and CEO of Republic. He brought with him the $125-million deal to buy Safecare and immediately began to analyze Republic's operations and strategy. For nearly a year, Martin commuted between Nashville and Dallas. Then in September, he moved the company, which he had renamed OrNda—to Nashville.

Martin had wanted to change Republic's name, which carried plenty of negative connotations. Just like NME became Tenet, Republic became OrNda. It was a name generated by Republic's public relations department—an Iroquois term, meaning "well-being." The word was so foreign to the hospital business that it immediately became the butt of jokes. (In Martin's defense, few of the investor-owned hospital companies can lay claim to having especially imaginative names. Former American Medical International President Royce Diener once quipped that a university professor told him his company's name was miserable because it consisted of nothing but adjectives.)

Not only did Martin change the company's name and headquarters, he switched strategies. He divested the company's previous diversifications, including surgery centers, clinical laboratories, and physician joint ventures. This move left Columbia alone on the road to physician ownership. At one point, Republic had joined Columbia in a crusade to make physicians partners in their hospitals. The two firms both buffeted critics and regulators who challenged the arrangements. Yet, Martin didn't want to fool with them, and unwound each of the physician partnerships.

In 1994, OrNda magnified its size with a three-way merger with two other hospital chains, American Healthcare Management (AHM) and Summit Health. AHM, another Dallas-based firm, was a fellow traveler in Chapter 11 with Republic. Summit was a small Burbank, California–based chain. The merger essentially doubled the size of Martin's company to 46 hospitals and $1.5 billion in annual revenues. Even more significant, OrNda began to command respect from Wall Street.

Like Columbia, OrNda began making some significant acquisitions of not-for-profit hospitals, although none drew quite the outcry as Columbia. OrNda was a smaller chain and never seemed like the oppressive bully that Columbia did. So, with little fanfare, it spent $122 million to buy St. Luke's Healthcare System, a not-for-profit facility in Phoenix, Arizona, and a large tax-exempt that was associated with Fallon Clinic in Massachusetts. Prior to his hiring in 1991, "Republic wasn't on anyone's scale of anything," Martin noted. When Martin sold it to Tenet in 1997, the chain drew a sale price of $3.1 billion—not a bad return on investment.

HEALTHSOUTH CORPORATION

Founded in 1984, HealthSouth is the nation's largest provider of rehabilitative healthcare with annual revenues of $2.2 billion and more than 1,000 hospitals, imaging centers, surgery centers, and other health facilities. The Birmingham, Alabama–based firm has a wide spectrum of services, including physical therapy, sports medicine, neurorehabilitation, occupational therapy, respiratory therapy, speech-language pathology, surgical services, and home healthcare. The company is the preeminent consolidator of rehabilitation services, both inpatient and outpatient. During 1995 and 1996, HealthSouth acquired a string of surgery center companies: Surgical Care Affiliates, Surgical Health Corporation, and Sutter Surgery Centers.

On its Web site, HealthSouth founder Richard Scrushy is described as "a modern American success story." In addition to building HealthSouth, Scrushy is an adviser to Speaker of the House Newt Gingrich as head of the Workers' Compensation

Reform Task Force and is a member of the Alabama Certificate of Need Review Board for the Alabama State Health Planning and Development Agency and Birmingham–Southern College's Board of Trustees. Scrushy was *Birmingham Business Journal's* 1996 "Man of the Year," and in 1994 he received the Arthritis Foundation's "Humanitarian of the Year Award."

From the rib of HealthSouth came another growth-minded healthcare company, MedPartners. The Birmingham-based firm is led by HealthSouth alumnus Larry House and is the nation's largest physician practice management firm. MedPartners became the premiere consolidator of physician practices, constructing a national network that had grown to 39 states by 1997. From Birmingham, the company's development officers fanned out across the country, methodically adding markets. For example, when Medpartners bought Talbert Medical Management Holdings in September 1997, the deal not only added to the company's presence in southern California and Phoenix, but added Salt Lake City/Provo, Tucson, and Albuquerque as new markets. Additionally, MedPartners also manages the nation's largest independent prescription benefits management company, dispensing 53 million prescriptions annually.

Interestingly, both HealthSouth and MedPartners became potential acquirers of Columbia's pieces after Frist took over in July 1997. HealthSouth was interested in the home healthcare business, surgery centers, and hospitals, whereas MedPartners was interested in Columbia's pharmacy benefit management business. Scott bought that business when it bought Value Health, which Frist decided to sell one month later. However, in a bolt from the blue, MedPartners in late 1997 decided to merge with Phycor, another physician company led by former HCA executive Joseph Hutts.

HEALTH MANAGEMENT ASSOCIATES

William Schoen had already engineered one turnaround when he was invited to join the board of Health Management Associates (HMA), a small, struggling hospital chain in 1983.

Before that, Schoen had successfully turned around a brewing company, F&M Schaefer, and sold it to Stroh Companies for $120 million. Accordingly, he retreated to Naples, Florida, for semiretirement.

Kent Dauten, a banker with First Chicago's venture capital division, brought Schoen into HMA and coaxed him to be co-CEO with the company's then top executive, Joseph Greene. Within two years, Greene was out, and Schoen was running the show.

Schoen repositioned the company to focus on rural markets where HMA could be the only hospital in town, or perhaps one of two. Hundreds of towns have that situation, and for the local hospital it amounts to a legal monopoly. Because of the previous debacles by National Healthcare, Westworld, and Gateway Medical (mentioned in Chapter 1), Wall Street shied away from rural hospital chains. However, rural hospital chains didn't go by the wayside; they just changed their stripes. They became "nonurban" hospital chains.

When HMA went public at $10 a share in 1986, the first sentence of the company's prospectus said the hospital chain provided "a broad range of general acute-care health services to rural communities." After doing a LBO in 1988, HMA went public again in 1991. This time the first sentence of the prospectus said the company provided "a broad range of general acute care health services in non-urban communities." Not much had changed, just the description. "Rural" didn't sound profitable enough, but "non-urban" did, obviously.

Yet, HMA is a good example of the fickle swings of Wall Street. Wall Street initially treated HMA poorly, lumping them in with other rural hospital chains that had historically treated Wall Street poorly. Analysts preferred to recommend the more cosmopolitan chains, such as Humana, NME, and AMI. Although HMA logged consistent profits, the company's stock never traded above its $10 per share offering price until mid-1988, and then it was only in the $11 range.

"It's in a bad industry," healthcare analyst Paul Szczgiel at Bear Sterns explained at the time. "They did a stellar job, but everybody kept wondering when something might break." So,

Schoen and his venture capital colleagues decided to take the company off the public market through an LBO. Even though hospital chains like Republic Health Corporation and Charter Medical Corporation were nearly strangled by the LBO debt they took on, HMA chugged along—business as usual. When the company went public again in February 1991, Wall Street was agog. The shares originally were priced at $13.50, but demand was so great that the price increased to $16.

"There's nothing different about the company," Schoen acknowledged at the time, when asked about the contrast in the company's demand from investors. For Schoen and his backers, the deal was wildly profitable. First Chicago and Prudential Venture Capital Management came away with a 400 percent profit in a little over two years. Both had kicked in $9.25 million to help finance the buyout in 1988. At the offering price, the stakes were now worth $51 million each. Since that time, HMA has continued to move along without stumbling. The hospital chain has few detractors and has managed to retain one of the cleanest reputations in the industry. Thanks to HMA and Healthtrust, investment bankers began saying good things about rural hospitals.

The tricky part about operating small-town hospitals is recruiting physicians. Doctors traditionally shun rural areas, but HMA has an edge in recruitment. By having a stable of rural communities to choose from, HMA can give physicians a number of locations from which to choose.

The chain's reputation is nearly spotless. The retired CEO of the nationally famous Mayo Clinic sits on HMA's six-member board (not exactly the kind of industry leader you'd expect governing an investor-owned hospital chain). HMA steered clear of many of the financial tactics used by other chains to get ahead. With equity and bank loans, the company has financed a steady growth pattern and accumulated the cash needed to bid for hospitals it really wants. While other hospital chains labor under debt-to-capital ratios for at least 40 percent and as much as 90 percent, HMA has kept its comfortable in the low teens—less debt expense, less cost, more profits.

That doesn't mean HMA executives always get what they want, though. Take, for example, Golden Triangle Medical Center in Columbus, Mississippi. This county-owned hospital received 11 offers from for-profit and not-for-profit groups once it decided to sell. Earl Holland, HMA's executive vice president, stood up at the county's board of supervisors meeting and said, "I'll give you $150 million." Recalled Charles Faulkner, the hospital's administrator, "Everybody's britches about fell off."

That offer seemed like an enormous sum in a town of around 30,000, yet the board of supervisors said, "no." Instead, the board took a lease offer from Baptist Memorial Healthcare Systems out of Memphis, Tennessee. That meant the community leaders also said "no" to an additional $800,000 in annual property taxes if HMA had bought the hospital. All of which goes to prove that for some people (especially in smaller communities) money isn't always the deciding factor.

Yet, there is every indication HMA towns are happy with their decision. In several cases, HMA built replacement hospitals for them, fueling civic pride in new multimillion dollar facilities.

QUORUM HEALTH GROUP

In a 1997 *Business Week* article, Quorum Health Group was described as a "kinder, gentler" Columbia. A stark comparison came in Ohio where both Quorum and Columbia initiated acquisitions of not-for-profit hospitals. Columbia blustered in, offending nearly everyone in its way. In one town, Columbia hired a hospital trustee prior to buying the hospital, which was a clear conflict of interest violation. Of course, all of the fault isn't Columbia's—what was that trustee thinking?

In response to Columbia's aggressiveness, the Ohio legislature passed a law designed to slow the acquisition process down. The attorney general's office was charged with reviewing the sale of charitable assets, such as hospitals. When Quorum bought two hospitals in the state in 1997, its officials had cordial relations with the attorney general's office. By contrast, when Columbia tried to buy a hospital in Massillon, Ohio, the attorney general's office blocked it. When Columbia tried to buy Blue Cross and Blue Shield of Ohio (which would have been a landmark deal), the attorney general's office again stood in the way.

The difference in style is notable because Quorum is actually a distant cousin to Columbia. In HCA's post-LBO divestiture days, the Nashville-based company spun off HCA Management Co., which was renamed Quorum. Quorum had contracts to manage not-for-profit hospitals that were owned by others. Frequently, the others were local governments. However, since its spin-off from HCA and subsequent public offering in 1994, Quorum Health Group has expanded into hospital ownership as well. In 1997, the company owned or leased 20 hospitals in addition to managing about 250 others.

Quorum is led by a core of former HCA executives who spent their early years driving down country roads where their customers, small, rural hospitals, were located. Although Quorum bought its first hospital in 1990, the company established itself as a true wheeler-dealer in 1993 when it bought 10 acute-care hospitals from Charter Medical Corporation for $340 million. Almost acting as a broker of hospitals, Quorum's President and CEO James Dalton kept just three of the 10. The rest were sold, closed, or traded in a series of transactions.

In May 1994, Quorum raised $100 million in its initial public offering. Quorum continues to be the largest manager of rural hospitals, however, and some of those hospitals became potential acquisition targets for the company.

Quorum is more than four times larger than its next competitor in the management business, Brim Healthcare, which is a subsidiary of Province Healthcare Co. Like Brim, virtually all of Quorum's managed hospitals are owned by tax-exempt organizations or governments. The average management fee is less than $200,000. With numbers like that, it's easy to see why many hospital companies don't fool with management contracts. It's much more lucrative to own hospitals than to merely manage them.

Managing hospitals in rural America is an interesting business, though, and it throws the company into the thick of small-town politics time and again. The management and strategic direction of Baylor University Medical Center in Dallas or Barnes Jewish Christian (BJC) Health System in St. Louis rarely makes the newspapers unless there's something dramatic. This is not so for a small county-owned hospital that's managed by a large out-of-town corporation.

Hospitals in small towns are often the largest employers, and if they are public hospitals, the board meetings are open to the community. Small-town newspapers, where eager "Woodward and Bernsteins" cut their teeth, are frequently ready to pounce on a hospital controversy. Indeed, Quorum has found itself in the midst of more than one.

For example, in the tiny town of Livingston, Texas, a ballot initiative on whether to increase tax support to a Quorum-managed hospital, Polk County Memorial Hospital, nearly split the community apart. In the weeks leading up to the May 1993 election, the semiweekly Polk County Enterprise was chock-full of stories, full-page advertisements, and letters to the editor from both sides. The opposition was organized and vocal. At one point, the group attacked two hospital executives for spending a whopping $946 to attend a two-day Quorum management meeting in Las Vegas.

W.O. "Zero" Lewis, a local resident who opposed the new tax, took out a full-page newspaper ad attacking the tax increase. "Polk Countians have been polarized by this Quorum plan and Quorum's political agenda," he charged. The vote failed. Nonetheless, Quorum has won tax elections in other small towns.

Understandably then, these types of management contracts aren't nearly as profitable as owning hospitals. Although other chains have bought more not-for-profit hospitals, Quorum hasn't been any slouch. It has the distinction of buying the first Baptist hospital ever sold to an investor-owned chain—Baptist Memorial Hospital in Gadsden, Alabama, for $70 million in 1993. The firm's most recent acquisition is a Methodist hospital in Mississippi.

One of its most interesting acquisitions was a Lutheran hospital in Fort Wayne, Indiana. Fort Wayne is a three-hospital town, and all three had been not-for-profit hospitals. The largest, Parkview Memorial, had a 40 percent market share, and the remaining 60 percent was split between Lutheran and St. Joseph Medical Center. At one point Lutheran officials were talking to their counterparts at St. Joseph about a merger, but negotiations broke down over clinical services that encompass religious issues, such as sterilization (a common deal-breaker in Catholic hospital mergers).

This situation presented a dilemma, though. Obviously, Lutheran couldn't merge with Parkview because the resulting 70 percent market share would draw a strong challenge from the Federal Trade Commission on antitrust grounds. If Lutheran wanted to join a system, and thereby gain the benefits of group purchasing, access to capital, and managed care expertise, it had to go outside Fort Wayne. Lutheran decided on Quorum, and the change was something new for Fort Wayne—a tax-paying hospital.

UNIVERSAL HEALTH SERVICES

Universal Health Services (UHS) operates 36 hospitals and another 30 ambulatory surgery and radiation oncology centers throughout the United States. In recent years, it has become more aggressive, expanding in both current and new markets. Two hospitals are under construction in markets where Universal already has a strong presence, and the company recently struck a deal with George Washington University Hospital. This is Universal's first District of Columbia hospital. Universal owns 80 percent of George Washington, a teaching hospital with a 150-year legacy in the community. Commenting on the arrangement, George Washington President Stephen J. Trachtenberg told an AP reporter in late September that George Washington talked with Columbia/HCA, but university officials feared that Columbia would not respect the hospital's teaching and research mission. Trachtenberg said, "Columbia struck us as predatory and UHS struck us as practical but accommodating." Since 1994 the company has added nearly a dozen hospitals and has become an appealing alternative to Columbia for tax-exempt hospitals looking for a buyer or joint venture partner.

Alan Miller founded Universal Health Services in 1978 after Humana, with a hostile bid, bought his previous hospital chain, American Medicorp. Universal stands apart from the other hospital companies in several ways. It is the oldest hospital chain with intact leadership.

The company is now the nation's third largest investor-owned hospital chain and is noted for its ability to be successful in competitive urban markets, such as Las Vegas. In 1997, UHS built a 148-bed acute care hospital in Summerlin, Nevada, just outside Las Vegas, which enhanced Universal's strength in one of the nation's fastest growing markets. UHS already owned Valley Hospital Medical Center, a 398-bed hospital in Las Vegas. The hospital has been one of UHS's most profitable facilities.

In addition, UHS opened a specialized women's health center in Edmond, Oklahoma in 1996, and will open two others in 1997—one in Oklahoma City and another in Austin, Texas. Regarding the recent brouhaha with Columbia/HCA and its effect on other for-profit chains, Miller was quoted in the aforementioned September AP article as saying, "I'm sick about it. Some people watch *60 Minutes* and they tend to lump us all together."

PROVINCE HEALTHCARE CORPORATION

Up until it decided to go public in the fall of 1997, Province was called Principal Hospital Company. However, there were a handful of other healthcare companies bearing the "Principal" moniker, so the hospital chain changed its name to Province.

Province is a rural hospital company that focuses on hospitals in towns with populations of 20,000 and up, markets that are just a tad smaller than those targeted by HMA. However, like HMA, Province looked for towns in which it could be the only hospital, in other words, the legal monopoly strategy.

Province leases or owns eight rural hospitals and manages another fifty through its subsidiary, Brim Healthcare. Province is kind of like Quorum because it has considerable interest in managing rural hospitals. It got into this business by purchasing one of the oldest hospital management companies, A.E. Brim & Associates.

Founder A.E. "Gene" Brim is one of the industry's pioneers, who began developing hospitals in 1963 with two partners. In December 1968, the partnership sold its three hospitals to American Medicorp, a firm that had been started just seven months earlier. It was the first acquisition for American Medicorp, which was scooped up in a hostile takeover by Humana in 1978. Brim initially stayed on to run the hospitals for Medicorp but left in 1971 because the company wasn't putting the promised capital into the facilities. He then started A.E. Brim & Associates, a consulting service that soon expanded into a management contracting company. "It was a product whose time had come," Brim declared.

By 1973, the company was managing five rural hospitals in the Northwest. In 1980, the fledgling firm, seeking a well-capitalized partner, was sold to a tax-exempt organization, Fairview Community Hospitals of Minneapolis. However, the Fairview partnership fell apart because Brim had increasing capital requirements, and Brim executives became impatient at the not-for-profit hospital's slow decision-making process. In 1984, Hillhaven, the nursing home subsidiary of NME, bought Brim, and both companies looked to expand into medium-sized and small communities. By 1986, Brim was also managing NME's 15 hospitals that were under management contracts.

In yet another restructuring at NME, the company sold Brim in 1987. Now part of Province, Brim manages 50 hospitals. Like Quorum, Province may be able to leverage management contracts into ownership stakes or leases, which are more profitable. With a squeeze in the Medicare payments that rurals are so dependent on, many make look to Province for cash to sell out.

PARACELSUS HEALTHCARE CORPORATION

A company that has struggled in the past year, Paracelsus may have been a one-time takeover target for Columbia/HCA. However, with Columbia/HCA's recent slowdown in acquisitions, Paracelsus's fate is much less certain.

The Houston-based firm is really two companies, which merged in 1996: Champion Healthcare Corporation and Paracelsus Healthcare Corporation. The company is managed by the executives of the former Champion, which was started in 1993, when Sprout, a venture capital arm of Donaldson, Lufkin & Jenrette, infused $91 million into a company led by a handful of seasoned hospital executives.

Many were former Republic Health executives, including President and CEO Charles Miller. Miller, as noted earlier in the book, was the man who turned down Richard Rainwater's offer to build a hospital company, a turn of events that led Scott and Rainwater to team up in forming Columbia.

Some regarded Champion as an early version of Columbia because it tried to build systems in a select group of markets. Until early 1994, Champion owned only a handful of hospitals in Texas and North Dakota; however, the year brought a burst of acquisitions and a merger with AmeriHealth, a small and financially struggling hospital chain. AmeriHealth's stock was traded on the American Stock Exchange. The merger gave Miller a quick and fairly inexpensive route to becoming a publicly traded company—a strategy Rick Scott also took when he merged Columbia with Smith Labs.

In addition to the merger with AmeriHealth, Champion bought a hospital in Salt Lake City from Columbia, and eventually built the largest system in Salt Lake, aside from the not-for-profit giant, Intermountain Health Care.

Paracelsus had a far different beginning. It was started by a German physician, Hartmut Krukemeyer, who bought the hospital subsidiary of the hotel corporation, Ramada Inns, in 1981. Krukemeyer remained sole owner until his death in May 1994 in Osnabruck, Germany. His son, Manfred George Krukemeyer, M.D., inherited the business and became the new owner.

In 1996, Paracelsus merged with Champion, forming a company with 28 hospitals and four skilled nursing facilities with 3,147 beds. Within a year, it restated its financial results back to 1991 and announced that it would sell or close PHC Regional Hospital in Utah. In the third quarter ending September 30, 1996, the company took one-time charges totaling $128 million related to the merger with Champion, bad debts, divestiture of its psychiatric hospitals, early repayment of debt, and divestiture of certain Los Angeles hospitals.

Paracelsus owns hospitals in the United States, Germany, Austria, England, Switzerland, and France, with more than 8,000 beds.

COMMUNITY HEALTH SYSTEMS

In 1982, the newly elected mayor of Troy, Alabama, Jimmy Lunsford, proposed that the city sell its hospital, Edge Regional Medical Center, a small facility with 97 beds. What was the reaction? "I was the biggest scoundrel in town," Lunsford proclaimed. Yet the new mayor thought it made sound economic sense. He reasoned that the city could sell the hospital at a profit and stop subsidizing the facility to the tune of about $500,000 a year. Even so, nobody wanted to give up their town hospital.

Twelve years later, Community Health Systems, a Nashville-based hospital chain, came to Lunsford with an offer to buy the hospital. Lunsford sat on it, mulling it over for two months without telling anyone. When he finally presented the proposal, there was "virtually 100 percent support" from the town of 15,000 residents. So what was different? Managed care was on the horizon. Edge Regional was progressively becoming emptier despite the town's best efforts to improve the physical plant and recruit physicians.

Recruiting doctors was the hardest part. "You can be in the nicest facility in the world, but if you don't have doctors . . ." Lunsford said, not finishing a sentence that had an obvious conclusion. In 1992 the hospital averaged 38 patients a day. One year later, the census had slipped to 35, and by 1994 the hospital averaged only 30 patients a day. Trustees could see the business slowly slipping away, yet the facility's high fixed costs remained the same.

Baptist Medical Center, located about 50 miles to the north, also had offered to acquire the hospital—for free. "They offered nothing," Lunsford noted. On the other hand, Community offered $14 million. Troy is the perfect example of a Community Health Systems hospital. Although the town's population is only 15,000, the hospital's service area is larger, at around 40,000. Even more important, Edge Regional is a sole community provider, which means there is no local competition. Community focuses on markets with populations ranging from 20,000 to 60,000. Of the chain's 40 hospitals, 26 are sole community providers.

Generally, Community acquires hospitals that have been getting about 30 percent of their healthcare dollars in town. It's not unusual for a rural hospital to get that much; the other 70 percent goes to hospitals in other larger towns or cities. "Our goal is to get 50 percent," says Deborah Moffett, Community's chief financial officer, until recently. One way to do that is to recruit more physicians. Rural physicians have always been notoriously hard to recruit, but like HMA, Community benefits from having several locations from which physicians may choose.

Although Community had been around since 1985, it hit the big leagues in 1994 when it bought Hallmark Healthcare Corporation. Formerly called National Healthcare, the company was a rural hospital chain. Community's purchase of Hallmark doubled the number of hospitals it operated to 40, spread throughout 17 states.

Community's story was enticing enough that the chain was snapped up by a private investment firm, Forstmann Little & Company, in 1996. The New York–based investment firm bought the chain in an all-cash offer and is likely to bring it public again in the next year or two. Obviously, Forstmann Little is looking for a big return on their investment, and time will tell whether the rural hospital business was good to its investors.

Right after that buyout, Community bought another small hospital chain, Dynamic Health. The Tampa-based chain had only managed to buy three hospitals in Texas, Louisiana, and South Carolina, before selling out to Community.

As this rather cursory review of other for-profit hospital chains highlights, Columbia/HCA is not the only player in the investor-owned healthcare sector. Nonetheless, Columbia/HCA is easily the most prominent. As Miller noted, the publicity surrounding the Nashville colossus has had an impact on all the for-profit chains. In actuality, the Columbia/HCA experience offers some valuable lessons for more than just the investor-owned providers.

7

Lessons Learned

In the fight between you and the world, back the world.

Franz Kafka

Some would argue that Rick Scott and his team at Columbia took on the venerable world of healthcare. Based on Kafka's observation, it was only a matter of time before the battle would take its toll on the innovative and aggressive firm Scott had assembled. However, given the enormity of the U.S. healthcare sector and its resistance to change, it's a wonder that Columbia got as far as it did before its momentum was slowed. The Columbia/HCA story is at once both fascinating and instructive. The lessons to be learned from Columbia's mercurial rise reach far beyond the healthcare industry. They are lessons that provide value to business students and professionals in every industry and at every level.

Despite all the media coverage of Columbia/HCA, little has been said about the lessons to be learned or the perspective of the "Monday morning quarterback" analysis. Few American companies offer such a rich and contemporary portfolio of both mistakes made and successes achieved. Given the backdrop of the entire for-profit healthcare industry, a few of these lessons are particularly instructive.

LESSON 1: ALLIES ARE ESSENTIAL, ESPECIALLY IN TOUGH TIMES

Scott and his team may have gleaned sound managerial advice from a Clark Gable classic. In the 1955 film *Soldier of Fortune,* Gable plays the part of a rogue who runs a smuggling operation out of communist China. Susan Hayward enlists Gable's assistance in finding and extraditing her husband, a photographer who has disappeared after a stint in Hong Kong. Early in the story Gable gains the favor of the villagers by giving them some of his smuggled goods, including wrist watches. In the final scene, as Gable escapes from communist China with his prize cargo, the photographer, he is pursued by a menacing host of communists, ready to fire on his ill-equipped vessel. Yet Gable is able to elude his pursuers with the help of hordes of Hong Kong fishermen who sail between Gable and the communists, all holding up their watches, grinning from ear to ear. The moral of the movie: When navigating foreign waters, make friends with the locals, so when times get tough they will intercede on your behalf. Scott and his team should have rented the video.

It could be easily maintained that from the outset, Scott and his associates at Columbia were sailing in unchartered waters. Certainly the concept they were championing had little precedent in the industry. Even though several of the executives at Columbia had prior healthcare experience, Scott had minimal experience in the massive industry—primarily putting together deals. The people with the most experience in running large companies backed by Wall Street were members of Scott's own board: Tommy Frist, Clayton McWhorter, and Donald MacNaughton. But by the time these individuals became involved with Columbia, Scott, Vandewater, and the Columbia/ HCA management team chose to mark their own course rather than seek advice from the well-versed veterans.

While assembling the colossal company, rather than make allies of non-Columbia veterans and experts within the industry, Columbia chose to challenge not only the status quo but the people who lived by the existing credo. In so doing, they set themselves apart from the industry, its opinion leaders, and its influence peddlers.

Their strategy seemed to work as long as the company was expanding, investors were happy, and the pursuers were out of sight. However, once the government started its investigation and the media launched its campaign, there were few industry allies to separate Columbia from its detractors and pursuers. In truth, with the exception of a sparse number of media commentators, such as Holman Jenkins Jr. with the *Wall Street Journal,* virtually no one came to Columbia's defense. Managers at Columbia had alienated so many people and organizations in their quest for rapid growth and industry dominance that the firm had few friends and consequently, few defenders. Granted, several Wall Street analysts stood by the company and continued to recommend the stock as a "buy," but their bullish backing did little to fend off the federal investigation or mitigate the (mostly) unfavorable media coverage.

Considering Columbia's aggressive approach and characteristic in-your-face competitiveness, the lack of supporters was not much of a surprise. In some industries, Columbia's aggressive behavior may have been acceptable (although even in more competitive industries, Columbia's constant flaunting of its size and superiority would have endeared it to few companies). Significantly, in healthcare, which is a historically collegial and only recently competitive industry, combative behavior is considered poor form to industry officials, community leaders, and high-profile industry observers. Jack Trammiel, the tough-as-nails former CEO of Commodore, is known for his comment, "Business is war." Even though healthcare is becoming more business oriented, the idea of "warfare" is still considered anathema in many circles.

Columbia knew its approach was atypical and incendiary, but that didn't seem to bother anyone in the core of senior management. In fact, their approach was part of the firm's modus operandi—and why not, the formula seemed to work. In a previous sporting era, Columbia could have been labeled the Jimmy Connors or John McEnroe of healthcare, in that it was young, brash, irreverent, and nonconformist. Yet while the company was successful, it fostered myriad followers and fans, including some healthcare "wanna-bes." Only when it stumbled did its many opponents come out of the stands to pile on the struggling maverick. As the old Hindu proverb states, "When an elephant falls, even the frog will kick it."

In an industry where over 80 percent of the hospitals are not-for-profit, Scott challenged the very viability of not-for-profit status, maintaining that such hospitals are "not good community citizens." He went public with his criticism, even to the point of publicizing studies in Florida and other states that demonstrated the superiority of the for-profit model from the standpoint of community contribution. The debate between Columbia and not-for-profit hospitals became so heated at one point that Richard Davidson, president of the American Hospital Association, had to act as mediator to calm the waters.

Such a strategy was not exactly a way to endear oneself or one's company to the established residents of the healthcare community. As noted previously, Scott further angered the largest segment of the industry and its leaders by calling not-for-profit hospitals, "tax-exempt" facilities. This rankled many not-for-profit hospital managers who had long considered their roles as major contributors to the community. Scott didn't seem to care about the reaction of his counterparts at not-for-profit facilities. He viewed them as competitors, not colleagues. Additionally, Scott insisted that his associates at Columbia use similar terminology in vocal and written communication. This attitude was underscored and later publicized by David Vandewater's oft-quoted remark made at a Columbia facility when he said, "You want to know who the enemy is? The enemy is St. Mary's. They've got your patients."

Such an overtly aggressive approach was bound to eventually backfire in healthcare. The healthcare industry is basically the largest "small" industry in America. Even though the healthcare contingent is massive, from a revenue standpoint (as well as number of employees) its informal control is under the auspices of a surprisingly small number of veteran executives—physicians and power brokers. Scott never quite broke into this circle. If anything, he violated its unspoken code of cordiality and disenfranchised himself and his organization from the group. That small group was tight with powerful allies; however, Scott didn't seem to care. He was focused on the market drumbeat resounding from New York's financial fiefdom, but healthcare is far too complex to focus singularly on one stakeholder group.

LESSON 2: MAIN STREET IS AS IMPORTANT AS WALL STREET

As noted earlier, Scott and his Columbia cadre were so focused on Wall Street that at times they seemed to ignore Main Street. Yet Main Street is a key audience in any business, including healthcare. In retrospect, Scott and his lieutenants overestimated the power and prominence of Wall Street, thus miscalculating the relevance and ramifications of perception by the folks on Main Street. Ironically, the investment community's assessment of a company will eventually be correlated to the perception of the public.

For some reason, Scott's Columbia/HCA team never seemed to fully grasp that simple principle. Indicative of that naivete were communications from Nashville following the federal investigations in El Paso and the broader investigative effort in July. On both occasions, the news from Nashville centered around the reaction of the investment community. As if breathing a collective sigh of relief, the press releases from Columbia corporate headquarters detailed the post-investigation support of the many stock market analysts who still felt Columbia/HCA was a "strong buy." Rarely, if ever, was there any market research delineating how the public perceived the news, or for that matter, any other stakeholder group. Throughout all the turmoil and the negative publicity there was little or no mention of how physicians, employers, or managed care executives were responding to the investigation.

If there was information about audience reaction (other than investment advisers), it was usually anecdotal. Noticeably lacking was sophisticated and meaningful market research that monitored reactions by the many stakeholder groups with which Columbia did business. This is not to say that there weren't efforts to communicate to various constituencies. Scott and Vandewater went on the road following the investigations to assuage employee, physician, and board member concerns. Otherwise, there didn't appear to be a cohesive and well-thought-out strategy for dealing with the potential backlash from the scrutiny (that came from the media as well as federal investigators). Had there been such an orchestrated strategy, perhaps events would have taken a different course, and the company not had to eventually resort to such drastic measures.

Focusing on only one or two audiences is always a risky strategy. In healthcare, it is particularly precarious because the industry is so dependent on the interaction of multiple stakeholder groups, including physicians, patients, community leaders, trustees, managed care executives, politicians, and business owners. The history of the for-profit firms in healthcare underscores the essential need to communicate to all these audiences, as well as the importance of measuring perception at all levels. Columbia never seemed too concerned about its perception among many of these groups. Columbia executives were determined to convey their message, even if audiences didn't want to listen. Although they were engaged in a great deal of communication, in many instances it was not interactive.

One case in point involved the Senior Friends program. Columbia had embraced the large program, which was designed as a way to get closer to the mature adult segment of the market. In marketing parlance, seniors would be termed the "heavy users," because they use such a large portion of healthcare services and account for a significant segment of the total healthcare dollars expended in America. Consequently, senior programs are not new to the industry, and Columbia's efforts were not all that innovative, except in scope and one particular facet.

Columbia executives, especially Scott, viewed Senior Friends as an effective and impressive vehicle to influence the political process. Consequently, a core component of each local chapter program was political activity, despite feedback that suggested that most seniors weren't all that interested in having their chapter serve as a forum for political activity. Fundamentally, most mature adults joined Senior Friends for the social component of the program.

Indicative of Columbia's failure to gauge the sentiment of the group was the national midyear convention of Senior Friends in 1997. Attempting to marshal the political potential of Senior Friends, the national conference was scheduled to be held in Washington, D.C., in the spring. The agenda called for an effort similar to that of the Columbia March Leadership Conference, intending to mount yet another impressive display for the folks on Capitol Hill. The conference was heavily promoted and was expected to draw thousands of Senior Friends from around the country. (At that time, total membership in the program was over 300,000.) There was just one problem: The event was scheduled on Mother's Day weekend. As one Senior Friends' chapter coordinator later commented, "Who in their right mind would schedule an event in Washington, D.C., involving mostly mothers and grandmothers on the *one* day they most want to be at home?" Predictably, the conference had sparse (just under 300) attendance and reduced success.

Such insensitivity to stakeholder sentiment was not atypical at Columbia. The corporate machine was unquestionably impressive when it came to generating communication; however, receiving communication and then acting on it was another story, unless, of course, the communication was in sync with the direction the company was headed. Negative or contradictory information and ideas were not solicited or encouraged. In many cases, they were ignored or brushed off as nonessential. Consequently, people within the organization quickly learned to sing the company song and keep a civil tongue when they held a contrary view. Compliance became more and more a hallmark of the firm as it grew larger.

LESSON 3: COMPLIANCE CAN HINDER AS MUCH AS HELP A COMPANY

As mentioned earlier, Columbia was moving in a direction of increasing compliance. In some areas, this was beneficial and economically efficient, such as the noted strategy of large-volume purchasing contracts. However, the downside of compliance is that it can seriously stifle creativity, innovation, and candid assessment of current operations.

This was becoming more the norm at Columbia under Scott's leadership. Executives quickly picked up on the reality that counter-opinion was not well-tolerated. Consequently, when ideas surfaced, a person with contrasting opinions (or even a devil's advocate) was viewed as a naysayer rather than a team player. Some of the ventures Columbia/HCA pursued in the final months of Scott's administration were arguably tangential and unquestionably time consuming. Observers have noted that many of these projects emerged as ideas that were never really evaluated under the microscope of reasonability and strategic fit. (In fact, many of these projects and programs were scrapped as soon as Frist and his new management team took over.)

The line by Jeff Goldblum's character of Ian Malcolm in the movie *Jurassic Park* may have applied to a few of the latter-stage projects at Columbia. At one point in the movie, Malcolm, the expert on chaos theory, challenges the developer of Jurassic Park with the observation, "Your scientists were so preoccupied with whether or not they *could,* they never stopped to think if they *should.*"

What could be done seemed to be the emphasis of the Columbia managers in Nashville. Indeed, the environment at Columbia during its go-go days (leading up to the time before the federal investigation and subsequent press-bashing) was characterized by a frenetic pace and a seemingly endless array of projects or programs. The perspective from the field—the hospitals that make up the colossus—was that no one individual or group was orchestrating the direction, so that each newly created division, department, or offshoot was vying for resources and efforts from the local facilities. This created a sense of frustration, a seeming lack of prioritization, and questions about strategic vision. The rapid-fire implementation approach could be termed "scatter-gun" strategy. "Let's throw out as many ideas, projects, and programs as we can. The winners will stick and the losers will sink."

One side of that strategy is appealing, perhaps even innervating. New ideas open opportunities and create a sense of electricity. Yet scatter-gun strategy, also termed "chaos management," requires a few critical elements within the organization: an established culture, the ability to pick and choose which initiatives work at the local level, and a willingness by upper management to listen to candid, constructive feedback from the field.

All of these elements were lacking at Columbia/HCA. For example, the company was assembled so rapidly that the culture couldn't keep up. (Frist himself noted several times after taking over for Scott, that Columbia was formed so fast that it didn't have time to put a culture in place.) Yet culture is essential for a break-neck pace, in that an imbedded culture allows employees and executives to weather the frenzy and to rely on each other. In essence, culture compensates for many mistakes and misgivings, and enables employees to meet the challenges with humor and humanity and to view the mistakes as learning opportunities, rather than dramatic failures.

Similarly, in a chaos strategy model, individuals and the organizations they represent need to be able to select what works best for their situation. If an opt-out alternative does not exist, each new day brings a new direction. Essentially, the most visible, politically-charged, or most recent initiatives become the tactic du jour. Such an approach creates confusion and frustration. As one dispirited executive stated, "The concept of 'they are all priorities,' is exhaustive and exasperating."

Columbia/HCA management didn't provide the option to selectively choose which initiative worked best at the local level. In essence, they were all priorities. The dizzying array of goals and areas of emphasis from Vandewater, Scott, and other members of senior management were overwhelming for many middle managers and senior executives. Some mumbled, others quit, but most doubled their efforts. With no distinction as to which projects were most important, the plate just kept piling higher with more tasks and fewer people to do them. The list of projects and initiatives got longer each month, with new departments or individuals adding one more "critical project" to the already unrealistically lengthy list. The "pedal faster" mentality began to take its toll as the light at end of the tunnel looked more and more like an oncoming train.

Scott, who was admired for his energy and drive and who loved to quote from famous people, may have benefited from a little-known quote by a well-known individual. Henry David Thoreau advised Americans to pursue a path of "Simplicity, simplicity, simplicity. Make your affairs two or three, not a hundred or a thousand." Columbia was definitely more on the path of pursuing a hundred or a thousand initiatives, rather than two or three.

LESSON 4: NEVER UNDERESTIMATE THE POWER OF THE PRESS

While the media may not have been the primary cause of Columbia's concerns, the constant barrage of negative publicity exacerbated whatever problems, perceptual and actual, the firm encountered. Many individuals felt much of the media maelstrom could have been avoided or at least downplayed had Columbia executives handled the press differently.

One senior marketing executive at the division level (who desired to remain anonymous) felt there were two defining points in Columbia's fall from grace. One of these was the *60 Minutes* segment on CBS in the fall of 1996. That segment, which painted Columbia in a less than favorable light, was arguably the first largely critical news story at a national level. The show focused on the Blue Cross merger in Ohio, but discussed some of Columbia's aggressive practices; however, as much as anything, the show highlighted the unwillingness of Columbia executives to talk to reporters (in this case Mike Wallace) and representatives from *60 Minutes*. As mentioned earlier, Wallace even closed the show with a rare retort to Lindy Richardson, senior vice president of marketing and public relations for Columbia, by calling attention to a fax Richardson had written just prior to the airing of the show.

The retort was rare, even for *60 Minutes*. As one high-level industry observer (who deals often with the press on healthcare issues) commented, "When have you ever heard of *60 Minutes* taking a dig at a VP of communications?" Wallace himself may have provided the rationale for such an unprecedented maneuver in an interview in *Modern Healthcare,* when he noted that in developing the Columbia segment, he had never been subjected to such an "orchestrated stonewall" in his many years of professional experience.

Based on discussions with other reporters and media accounts, such orchestrated stonewalling was not all that atypical with the Columbia contingent. For whatever reason, Columbia management seemed to be averse to media, if not antipathetic toward members of the press—more so as the tension increased and the investigation efforts intensified.

However, such a posture was not always the case. In the earlier days of Columbia (during the early 1990s and even up to about 1994), Rick Scott and Columbia representatives would often talk to reporters and go on record with statements about everything from Columbia's expansion plans to commentaries on the national healthcare reform movement. In truth, it may have been some of those comments about healthcare reform or other statements, like David Vandewater's "We aren't in the healthcare business; we're in the sick care business," which was often cited out of context, that led the senior management of Columbia to be more media shy and less willing to discuss plans or philosophy with members of the press.

This latter attitude may have resulted in the perceived attempt at stonewalling cited by Wallace, which may have been little more than a heightened cautiousness caused by past misrepresentation. Whatever the case, the resulting effect left a sense that Columbia would not answer the questions posed and would not provide the story desired.

The rule of thumb in media relations is never let the press default to the story being told without your comments. In other words, if the company doesn't provide the information, the press will go elsewhere to find it. Usually the other source is far less favorable than getting it straight—even if it's less than polished—from the company itself. Columbia executives didn't seem to understand that basic principle and were surprised when the press came to conclusions about the firm, even though Columbia wasn't willing to provide its side of the story.

Some objective observers have wondered, for example, why prominent publications like *USA Today, The New York Times,* or *The Wall Street Journal* would rely on partisan and disgruntled sources like Peter Young or Marc Gardner. The answer is Media Relations 101. If a company doesn't provide meaningful and timely response, the press will seek out other sources. Astute media relations staff and consultants know that "no comment" is always unwise and usually dangerous, as it merely piques media interest. Recognizing the incomparable value of a sound public relations strategy, Columbia/HCA (under Frist) hired Burson Marsteller, the well-known PR firm, in the autumn of 1997. Even more important than that move, however, was senior management's open attitude toward the press. Consequently, the tone and frequency of articles about Columbia changed dramatically.

Columbia's problems with the press may have been a manifestation of a more fundamental managerial hang-up—namely the need to control. As Columbia/HCA grew to behemoth size, there was parallel growth in its controlling instincts. Nowhere did that play out as visibly as with the media. Columbia executives, by their actions, demonstrated that if they couldn't control what the media reported, then they wouldn't even participate. Rather, they chose to launch a counteroffensive with the mega–million-dollar branding campaign. This latter strategy revealed a surprising naivete (for a $20 billion company) as well as a misunderstanding of how the public assesses its information.

The naivete that Columbia exhibited sprang from the notion that a company or individual can "control the press." This is (thankfully) a rare occurrence in America, especially for corporations. Through a synchronized and sophisticated effort of frequent communication, openness, mutual respect, and willingness to admit mistakes, it is possible to perhaps "manage the media," but not control it. Columbia executives didn't seem to, or didn't want to, understand that elementary principle.

Consequently, the firm opted to communicate its message through paid media with its unprecedented and unparalleled branding campaign. The pursuit of this initiative, however, revealed a basic misunderstanding of how the public rates and receives its information. Most Americans realize that advertising is patently partisan. That's okay, as long as the scripted message agrees with the more nonpartisan view of the media. When the two diverge, however, the public is more likely to believe the more objective (by definition) source of information—namely the press. In Columbia's case, the relentless advertising probably exacerbated the negative commentary by the press because of the stark contrast between what the media was reporting and what the branding campaign was purporting. In essence, each ad was more of a reminder than a rejoinder of the critical coverage by the press.

The history of American business is rife with anecdotes of major companies, from Exxon to General Motors, that failed to communicate effectively with the public through the media. In some cases, it was arrogance; whereas in others, it was a function of animosity toward the press. Despite the reason, the result is often the same: The company loses and loses big. Yet for the many incidents of American businesses that have lost favor in the public's eye and value from the investor's viewpoint, Columbia will likely go down as the firm that took the biggest hit from the media and suffered the most at the hands of reporters. They might have taken a different approach had

Columbia handled their relations with the press in a more co-operative and informative fashion.

LESSON 5: SET REALISTIC GOALS

The ambitious goals that Columbia executives set for their managers and employees have received considerable press. As the company's growth options through acquisitions or mergers began to diminish, the operational and financial targets began to expand—to unrealistic proportions. there were two basic problems with the targets (known as "stretch goals"): First, they were not developed in an interactive process—they came down from "the mountain," or in this case, out from Nashville. Second, they were increasingly based more on zeal than on reality.

A good example of this was highlighted at the Senior Friends coordinators conference in Nashville in the early summer of 1997. As one of the market coordinators for Senior Friends tells it, the conference featured a speech by Vandewater. In the course of his rather informal give-and-take with the audience, he picked up on some grousing about the Senior Friends membership targets for the year. (Senior Friends had started the year with about 300,000 members, and Columbia corporate had established a goal of hitting 1,000,000 members by New Year's Day of 1998; consequently each hospital or division had a proportionately unrealistic target, upon which part of the coordinator's incentive bonus was based.) In a move to appease the audience and validate the concept of stretch goals, Vandewater acknowledged that the goals were ambitious, but maintained that lofty goals are what brings out the best in individuals and organizations. Furthermore, others could learn from those who hit their targets. Then, to prove his point, he asked for a show of hands of those who were on course to hit their individual market goal. Not one hand was raised.

As the stretch goals took on herculean dimensions, they became more exposed to media scrutiny and internal dissension. Part of the media scrutiny hinged on the idea that such unrealistically high financial targets may have contributed to some of the irregular and questionable behavior for which Columbia was being investigated. Another component that drew media attention and public concern was the emphasis on cost control (as manifested by reduction of staff), which was correlated to hitting the stratospheric financial targets required of Columbia managers. At the same time, the goals became a more pronounced focal point for frustration, if not derision, as local admistrators and their senior advisors realized how increasingly unrealistic the targets were becoming.

The upside to the stretch goals mantra was the strategic planning process that encouraged executives to start thinking outside the box and consider other options for growth, such as long-term care, alternative medicine or health and wellness centers. However, these were projects and prospects that required a lengthy germination period before the initiatives could produce meaningful results. So in reality, they offered little perceived relief to the pressured executives. As mentioned earlier, frequent and focussed communication regarding the lofty targets was relayed to Tommy Frist and was one of the chief reasons (that he cited) for taking the eventual action of removing Scott and Vandewater.

To only note the miscues would be a grave disservice to the drive and accomplishments of the Columbia leadership. The reality remains that Rick Scott, David Vandewater, and the other executives at Columbia/HCA accomplished a great deal in a short time. Much can be learned from these accomplishments, as well as from the failures. Whoever merits a listing on the prestigious list of *Time* magazine's "Twenty-Five Most Influential People" is worth regarding and perhaps emulating.

LESSON 6: TRADITIONAL PROBLEMS OFTEN REQUIRE A NONTRADITIONAL APPROACH

Anyone with a memory would agree that just a few years ago healthcare was bogged down with the weight of its own operational baggage. In the aftermath of Columbia's floggings by the press and the investigations by the government, too few people remember that less than five years ago healthcare was on the ropes. The industry was seriously under fire because of rising costs and insufficient access. The ill-fated reform initiative launched by the Clinton Administration in 1994 proved once and for all that the American public did not want to turn the problem over to the federal government.

Still, American industry was in a dither about healthcare costs. Employers were screaming about double-digit health inflation rates, arguing that spiraling benefits costs were eroding productivity and threatening to undermine their ability to compete in a global economy. Consequently, when Rick Scott stepped up to the plate with a businesslike prescription for the notoriously non–business-oriented industry of healthcare, he was lauded by the commerce community.

Columbia was viewed as the hospital company that took costs seriously. Scott proclaimed that the Columbia system would be economically efficient, thus making it more attractive to the purchasers of health services, as well as appealing to the equally cost-centric managed care companies that acted as financial intermediaries for the nation's employers. Scott recruited physicians to walk by his side and invest at his side, with the belief that physicians and hospitals should have aligned incentives— financial as well as philosophical. Scott's rationale was that once physicians realized how much they drove up the cost of healthcare, they would be more likely to be cost focused also.

In fact, physicians have a large stake in the cost effectiveness (or lack thereof) of individual hospitals, as well as national healthcare costs. Even though hospitals account for over 40 percent of the outlays to the healthcare industry, the axiom in the industry is, "the most powerful tool for cost control in the U.S. is the physician's pen." Physicians are the ones who order tests, admit patients, and perform surgeries. Hospitals are merely the places where physicians practice their trade.

Therefore Scott's approach to healthcare was focused and financially sound. His concept of running hospitals and other health institutions with business acumen and measurable results was anticipated and applauded by those who paid the tab. However, to say that Scott and Vandewater's vision was constricted to merely a concentration on cost and operational efficiency would be misleading, as well as a misrepresentation of the overall value of their contribution. Columbia was pushing the borders on many fronts, and this was a much needed exercise in a change-resistant environment.

LESSON 7: CHANGE AGENTS AREN'T WELCOME, BUT THEY ARE NECESSARY

As Columbia prospered and became more prominent, Scott became more comfortable with his role as a change agent. It may have been this realization that provided him with a driving sense of purpose and enabled him to weather the mounting criticism. What was noted earlier as an inattentiveness to other audiences may have in fact been self-securing intellectual insulation against those who might distract him from his course. In other words, the fact that he didn't seem to heed the warnings and suggestions of others may have been his way of coping with his role as a maverick who challenges the status quo. As the saying goes, "The bull in the china shop may be unwelcome, but he does not go unnoticed."

The very nature of a change agent is to challenge and be challenged. Healthcare needed a company like Columbia for many reasons. First, as mentioned in the preceding section, the system was too costly and was dysfunctional. Part of the reason for this was the inherently complex (and arguably flawed) duality financing of American healthcare (discussed later in Chapter 8). Just as significant is the organizational structure of healthcare, which is basically America's last large cottage industry. Among other things, this nation's healthcare system has been called vast and inchoate, which is a very accurate portrayal of at least the hospitals in the country. This disorganization and fragmentation means that elements that exist in other industries are lacking, such as capital for research and development, sufficient market research for diversification, and adequate consideration of advanced techniques and procedures to modify existing approaches.

Most hospitals and healthcare systems are too undercapitalized to finance the kind of expansion or even exploration of new concepts, practices, or markets that provide much needed revenue infusion. Consequently, the hospital industry has had very little real growth over the past decade. Much of the increase in total revenues for the hospital sector has come from price increases—not from new services, expanded markets, or diversified products.

Columbia/HCA was the beacon in the night for an industry adrift in the sea of tried and true. The problem with the financial waters that hospitals navigate is that from a revenue standpoint, the tried and true are more the stagnant and stale. Columbia was charting new oceans. In a sense, Columbia was not just a change agent, it was an agent of "sea change."

Never before had a company amassed the capital clout and financial backing to pursue the ventures Columbia was proposing. At one point in time, Columbia was so financially strong that the path to continued growth seemed endless. However, the capital backing didn't just translate into acquiring new hospitals.

One of the unintentional benefits of Columbia/HCA's forced slowdown in mergers and acquisitions (as all the big and available fish were in the boat, so to speak) was that top management had to turn its attention to other avenues for revenue growth. This focus produced some innovative and intriguing combinations and permutations. Some of these, like the home health integration, which Frist took no time divesting, may have been a lightning rod from an investigative standpoint, but the strategy of integration (vertical as well as horizontal) remained a viable consideration. Columbia's foray into ambulatory surgery centers was innovative and in sync with market trends. Who could argue with the idea of moving more patients to outpatient surgery with shorter stays? The idea was both more economical and preferable from the patient's viewpoint; after all, patients would much rather be home in five hours than in five days. Not many people relish the idea of staying in a hospital when their home is the option.

However engaging these ventures were, they were not as much on the vanguard as some of the less-publicized initiatives Columbia was launching or considering. Columbia was expanding in international markets. Granted, AMI and other companies had attempted to go international in the 1980s, with some success. Yet Columbia, with its unparalleled resources and its purchasing clout, may well have tapped into markets that other industries have found to be the godsend for declining products and services in America. The world has changed considerably since HCA and AMI ventured into the foreign market, and American healthcare has much to offer and to learn from its counterparts in Europe, Asia, and the developing nations of the globe.

Columbia/HCA knew that information technology was not only the future of American industry, it was the future of healthcare. Yet the healthcare industry has historically lagged behind the rest of the nation by about five years in its acceptance and application of computer technology. Columbia was out to set the standard for the entire industry and be on par with other leading companies in all sectors of the business community. Experts have long wondered (and rightly so), with all the medical advances available to American physicians, caregivers, and the patients they serve, why the information component of healthcare can't keep pace with the clinical aspects of the industry. Columbia appeared ready to spend the required capital and the time necessary to integrate information technology among the physician, nursing station, managed care payor, and whatever party was essential to the transaction. Small hospitals with limited budgets couldn't even dream of the kind of information integration Columbia was considering and establishing for the industry.

Perhaps the component of healthcare (especially hospitals) that is most lacking and deserves the greatest attention is the notion of research and development—not clinical research, but business application and new product research and development. Columbia was about to launch several initiatives that would distance it from all its competitors, both for-profit and not-for-profit, in terms of new fields of exploration. With the addition of Dr. Herbert Wong to the senior management team, Columbia had obtained his cadre of colleagues at the former consulting firm of Quantum Solutions. This group was developing plans for evaluating everything from alternative medicine to consumer goods.

While a research and development division is a staple in most industries, it is basically nonexistent in the hospital industry. Consequently, hospitals and physician groups have rarely ventured beyond the traditional offerings, and when they have, the results have been disastrous. In the 1980s some hospitals tried to diversify by offering catering services, laundry services, and other tangential programs that drained resources and produced little revenue.

Columbia had a need to grow. Whereas necessity is the mother of invention, in Columbia's case it proved to be the mother of expansion and exploration. Had this effort taken flight, as with so many other Columbia initiatives, it undoubtedly would have spawned myriad imitators, and the industry likely would have gained great benefit from the exercise of diversification.

LESSON 8: THERE IS AN UPSIDE TO LOFTY GOALS

The concept of Columbia's much-maligned stretch goals was reviewed earlier; however, there was definitely an upside to the ambitious goals that Scott and Vandewater established for their employees. Admittedly, the goals were taking on a frenzied life of their own, but they were also the catalyst for some impressive achievements.

One of those achievements was the Web site. In a very brief time span, Columbia was able to bring its view to the outside world on the Internet. With relatively few resources and little more than incredible drive, the Columbia team constructed a Web site that not only gained high marks among heady competition like the Mayo Clinic, but was the recipient of phenomenal activity. One particular program, a physician chat session, received more hits than any other interactive session, with the exception of Michael Jackson's much-ballyhooed online chat.

In creating its highly visible site, Columbia galvanized the industry into action in a medium that is becoming one of the most engaging environments for the sharing of health information. Columbia may not have been first, but it was rapidly becoming (and still is, since the Web site is still quite active) one of the most prominent healthcare sites in the country.

Another area in which Columbia received favorable and much-deserved notoriety is its information services. As noted earlier, the goal of the company was to link the vast array of stakeholder groups through the medium of information technology. In fact, Columbia's information services department was ranked as the most effective user of information technology by *Information Week* in September of 1997 for its rapid and thorough implementation of information technology. The healthcare colossus was in good company, ranking ahead of General Electric, Lockheed Martin, General Motors, and International Paper.

Mentioned in an earlier chapter was the concept of best demonstrated practices. The focus on clinical practices provided an avenue for a potentially valuable and certainly innovative role for hospitals. For-profit hospitals have historically been the factories, so to speak, for medical technology, but not the laboratories. Columbia was pushing the envelope by creating a mechanism for testing new advances and partnering with pharmaceutical firms, physician groups, and academic centers in exploring new technologies and advances. Much of the effort was being led by Tucker Taylor and Herb Wong, whose charge included disease management.

The list goes on and on. Unfortunately, in the aftermath of the federal investigation few of these endeavors have even been mentioned, let alone spotlighted. Yet the need for a company with financial clout to expand the industry's operational borders and challenge traditional thinking and methodology is something that could benefit the nation and support the industry. The

Health Care Advisory Board, a highly respected research group out of Washington, D.C., known for publishing reports about leading hospitals and health systems, produced a report on the for-profit industry. The report, "The Rising Tide," focused primarily on Columbia. The notion was that a rising tide raised all boats, and the theme of the research was that systems like Columbia were raising the bar for American hospitals with efficiency as well as system design. The program was one of the best-attended and most sought-after reports the company produced. Ironically, the events of 1997 would probably leave an indelible imprint in the public's mind that Columbia, rather than raising the tide, had been caught in a tidal wave. The lesson to be learned from the summer of 1997 is perhaps the most relevant for this topic, which is that healthcare is unlike any industry in America.

LESSON 9: HEALTHCARE IS TRULY UNIQUE

In any other industry, Rick Scott and his hard-driving colleagues would likely be admired rather than vilified. Terms like *aggressive, profitable, workaholic, competitive,* and so forth, are an integral part of the business community vernacular, but not so in healthcare.

Healthcare, especially hospital management, is truly an American original; however, the problem for Scott was that it is also an American atypical. Tactics employed by companies such as IBM and Microsoft are viewed as outlandish in healthcare. Scott believed that approaching healthcare in a more businesslike fashion would not only prove good for Columbia and its shareholders, but would be good for America. If not, he reasoned, the market would vote. Ultimately, from Scott's vantage point, the market's determination of Columbia's value was what would drive Columbia to do the best and be the best. This reasoning cannot be challenged on many fronts, and has certainly worked for most of America's leading industries. However, what Scott may not have realized, as few people do, is that healthcare is definitely different.

Healthcare in this country defies definition and comparison. People who want to compare it to the airlines, banking, or any number of service industries in America usually fall short. The reason is almost too obvious. Healthcare involves human life. Other large industries involve significantly less intense transactions or events.

No other sector of America evokes such strong emotions as the healthcare industry. In fact, Dick Davidson, American Hospital Association president, doesn't even like to refer to healthcare as an industry. He believes such a moniker diminishes the value and the unique nature of its character. In some respects he is absolutely right, and based on the Colombia experience, his preference may prove even more accurate.

Had Rick Scott done what he and his associates did in another industry, would he have come under fire by the media, investors, or any of the groups that are now attacking the giant hospital company? In most industries aggressiveness is viewed as healthy and even necessary. Competition is just a part of the capitalist fabric. If IBM lays off several thousand employees in a move to streamline its costs and improve its efficiency, people empathize, but the news vanishes after a day or two. Yet if a hospital chain or an individual hospital lays off several workers to account for declining revenues, the community and the press are in an uproar. Engineers are one thing; caregivers are quite another. In essence, the concept of a business approach was unquestionably sound, but given the industry and the sensitivity to such an approach to a venerable industry, the execution was precarious.

8

CHAPTER

Implications

I doubt that, long-term, the Columbia name will be the
name of the company.

Vic Campbell, October, 1997

For all the media attention given to Columbia and the massive
Medicare investigation, precious little has been written about
the impact or implications of the entire affair. Healthcare is a
volatile field, and this type of attention and accompanying publicity will have significant ramifications for the nation and several subgroups. Whether aware or not, the government and the
press have launched an initiative that will dramatically affect
perceptions, reimbursement, and the organizational infrastructure of American healthcare. Such a prediction is borne from
historical precedent, for whenever the government intervenes in
the nation's healthcare delivery system, it has produced rever-
berations that have altered the manner in which we view and
receive these critical services.

IMPLICATIONS FOR AMERICA

Winston Churchill was once asked to comment on the direction of Russia (in the late 1930s). His famous response was "I cannot forecast to you the action of Russia. It is a riddle wrapped in a mystery inside an enigma." Were Churchill alive today, he might say the same thing about the American healthcare system. Its complexity is baffling, and its enormity is overwhelming.

Consequently, developing a meaningful solution for solving "America's healthcare crisis" (as it was termed during the Clinton reform campaign) is like trying to defeat IBM's chess-playing computer, *Deep Blue*. The best one can hope for is a draw—a short-term respite from the inevitable. The brief history of American healthcare is filled with well-meaning but only temporarily effective solutions. Too many times the probable solutions are crafted by individuals with insufficient understanding of the system's complexity and inadequate resources to offer long-term solutions. The result has empirically been overly simplistic solutions that either transfer the problem, without really resolving it, or wear thin with time, giving way to an even larger dilemma. The fundamental challenge can be distilled down to two components that do not lend themselves to equitable or lasting resolution: financial duality and philosophical disagreement.

FINANCIAL DUALITY

The U.S. healthcare system is as economically polarized as it is complex. While the majority of payments for healthcare come from the private sector, over one-third of the costs are covered by government outlays (in the form of Medicare and Medicaid). This duality of private and public financing has created a vastly complex, high-stakes game of seesaw economics, wherein one financing body's actions have a counterbalancing effect on the other. Achieving equilibrium for both parties has been problematic. Four defining movements in healthcare history substantiate this disequilibrium theory.

A. Post–World War II healthcare benefits legislation

Much of the dualistic nature of healthcare and the subsequent polarization can be traced to the legislation that was passed shortly following the end of WWII. The federal government had imposed a wage and price freeze. Like all wage and price freeze enactments in this country, the aftereffects were detrimental. This incident was no exception. As a salvo to business, tax legislation was passed that allowed corporations to offer healthcare benefits to their employees without the employees incurring any taxable consequences. Thus began the mammoth movement in the United States to have corporations underwrite the healthcare insurance and benefits of the large majority of American workers. To this day, American corporations write the biggest check for healthcare payments in the nation. Given that it was in direct response to a wage and price freeze, the astute student of economic history can understand that the program got started on the wrong foundation.

B. Medicare

The notion of corporations picking up the tab for health benefits and insurance coverage worked for about 15 years, with minimal involvement from the government. Then, observing the inequity for those who retired from the work force and others outside the corporate mileu, politicians proposed that the federal government needed to intercede and see to the needs of the underserved and underprivileged. In 1965, sweeping legislation was introduced that would ensure that older Americans would have the same peace of mind (in terms of healthcare coverage) afforded working Americans and their families. Medicare legislation was a good idea, the scope of which was vastly underestimated and the reimbursement structure inherently flawed.

Medicare was based on cost-plus reimbursement, which meant that organizations had little incentive or motive to control costs. As Pulitzer Prize–winning author Paul Starr noted (in his book, *The Logic of Health Care Reform*), "From the beginning the recipe was a formula for disaster." Although the disaster took a while to manifest itself, the massive buildup of the nation's healthcare machine was to eventually produce the overcapacity dilemma the nation now faces. As noted earlier, Medicare was also the catalyst for the development of the for-profit healthcare sector in America.

C. *Diagnostic-Related Groups (DRGs)*

Less than 20 years after Medicare was passed, the costs of the program were threatening to drain the nation's coffers. Harking back to a strategy implemented on so many other occasions, the government resorted to its own internal price ceiling. Developed by researchers at Yale, the prospective payment system (PPS) was introduced into the healthcare vernacular with the concept of diagnostic-related groups (DRGs). As noted earlier, these 480+ DRGs placed a cap on the amount hospitals would receive for various procedures. This dramatic change in reimbursement had a sizeable impact on hospitals. In a very brief span of time, hospitals were forced to become efficient providers of care or suffer the economic consequences.

The impact on private financing was predictable. Given the volatile nature of healthcare financing, many hospitals merely shifted the costs from insufficient Medicare funding over to the private side. This meant higher bills for corporations. By the late 1980s employers were decrying the escalating costs. This drumbeat of dissension (which was also echoed by employees who started to share in the burden of higher costs) was heard by politicians in the early 1990s and resulted in the ill-fated, but highly publicized reform campaign.

D. *Managed Care*

Industry didn't wait for the government to resolve the problem. Managed care companies (health maintenance organizations [HMOs] and preferred provider organizations [PPOs]) increased their visibility and offered employers predictable rates and lower increases in overall costs. Employers liked the offer, and managed care experienced a growth spurt from less than 5 percent (total U.S. enrollment) in the mid-1980s to over 25 percent by the mid-1990s.

Government's eventual reaction to managed care was to embrace it. Executives at the Health Care Financing Administration (HCFA) had gone on record saying that they would try to move more Medicare and Medicaid recipients into the HMO programs. This was the probable (and market-based) solution to the problem of rapidly increasing healthcare costs. However, that was before the federal investigation into Medicare abuse. Now the government appears to have chosen a regulatory solution over a market-driven solution. This approach marks a major departure for the government and could be a significant harbinger of a shift in American perception and policy.

Clearly, forces in the federal government are responding to research that reveals many Americans (especially the elderly) believe the primary reasons for rising healthcare costs are fraud and abuse. By focusing on providers and the alleged abuses of the system, the government is back in the picture of resolving the healthcare dilemma, only this time they are swimming with the tide of public opinion.

However, the flip side of that direction can be paraphrased by Albert Einstein's famous maxim, "You cannot simultaneously prepare for war and peace." In the case of the federal government, it may not be able to simultaneously move toward a market-driven model (as with the drive for increased HMO enrollment) while increasing the regulatory oversight. The two strategies seem incongruent but indicative of the philosophical disagreement within the nation regarding the true nature of healthcare, which is the second significant barrier to a lasting and meaningful solution.

PHILOSOPHICAL DISAGREEMENT

There are basically two schools of thought in America regarding the optimal configuration of the nation's healthcare system. One side argues for the market-driven model, with costs being controlled through efficient supply and demand and all the principles of standard commodity economics. The other school of thought argues for a national healthcare system, like that found in most industrialized nations. In the latter model, private healthcare is reserved for those who are willing and able to pay extra. This model has a minority of backers, although the healthcare reform movement of the early 1990s revealed that its numbers are growing.

Yet even within the ranks of those who desire a market-driven model, there is divergence of thought regarding the true nature of healthcare. Much of the nation (as determined through sophisticated polling) believes that receiving basic healthcare is a right. The problem lies in how to finance this "right." Most of the population is content to leave financing up to the private sector, but someone or some entity has to ensure that the underserved and underpriviledged do not slip through the net. All of this leads back to the financial duality and inter-connection between the financial and philosophical issues. Obviously, the current investigation of the healthcare industry has a significant impact on the debate.

IMPLICATIONS FOR THE HEALTHCARE INDUSTRY

Richard Davidson, president of the American Hospital As-sociation (AHA), knew very well the consequences of the fed-eral investigation into Medicare billing, which was aimed largely at Columbia, but which affected the industry he repre-sented. The impact, as he noted, could produce an erosion of confidence in the hospital industry. He also knew that hos-pitals did not need that erosion of trust at this point in time. He has observed what such a crisis had done to the managed care industry.

Davidson and other industry leaders realized that one of the disappointing outcomes that could emerge from this debacle surrounding the intense scrutiny of billing practices is what could be termed as "the junior high syndrome," a basic strategy of remaining inconspicuous within the industry. In other words, a healthcare organization won't do anything that would call at-tention to an organization or an initiative. Why stand out if it brings so much scrutiny?

This would be a tragedy. Healthcare needs bold leadership and it desperately needs innovation. The industry is already known as a "lemming" industry, where far too many hospitals and systems follow the latest trend, proven or not. The next few years will mark extremely difficult times for healthcare in America. The government will continue to cut back on Medicare payments, regulation will increase, and the managed care movement will reduce payments to physicians and hospitals. In this time of decline, the industry cannot afford to take a "stay in your seats" mentality. In truth, the negative publicity Columbia has received will filter down to most hospitals, whether they are for-profit or not. As Rick Wade, senior vice president of communications for AHA, noted in a September issue of *AHA News,* "We've got to begin to stop the finger-pointing and make some progress. The fact of the matter is the current administration has put in place a bounty system, and members resent this."

Every few years brings a new entity non grata in the healthcare industry. In the 1980s, that entity was the insurance companies. In the early 1990s, the pharmaceutical firms were seen as the problem. In the mid-1990s, managed care companies were the culprits. Now, as Dick Davidson feared, hospitals could take that role, which would be a double whammy for the hospital industry. Already reeling from insufficient (and declining) re-imbursements, a challenge to the character of the institutions would be too much for many individuals and institutions to bear. Hospitals have always been seen as havens, where caring people can administer to health needs and also extend a hand to support groups, families, friends, and so on. If these basic tenets are challenged, hospitals will feel the effect for years to come.

One of the interesting barometers to watch will be the impact on cost. During the second quarter of 1997, the healthcare price index revealed that healthcare inflation had climbed a mere 0.3 percent or two points lower than general inflation. Yet, as noted earlier, whenever the government has intervened in healthcare policy or financing, the impact on healthcare costs has been dramatic. The most telling, recent example of this was the double-digit inflation increases of the late 1980s, caused (as some experts estimate) by hospitals' and other health organizations' costs shifting from the capped Medicare payments (through DRGs) over to the private sector. The recent investigative effort by the government to rein in fraud and abuse comes at a time when healthcare spending is (for the most part) under better control than ever before in recent history.

The effect on overall costs will be interesting to watch, especially since the increased investigation will likely produce increased overhead (at the facility level) for compliance procedures, regulatory training, and increased staff to monitor the activities and policies of the hospital. Perhaps the greatest cost will come in the form of opportunity costs—namely, hospitals' unwillingness to pursue innovative and intensive efforts to squeeze costs out of the system. This overly conservative approach may rule the day because of a fear of violating regulations under the increased scrutiny of federal overseers.

IMPLICATIONS FOR THE FOR-PROFIT SECTOR

There is no doubt that the investigation and the negative publicity has had and will continue to have an unfavorable impact on the entire for-profit industry. It will affect some more than others, but the group will never be viewed quite the same. In fact, research by the Kaiser Foundation highlighted quantitatively the negative impact of the Columbia/HCA probe and noted that the for-profit hospitals had received reduced marks in categories such as quality of care, efficiency, and value to the community. Public Opinion Strategies conducted research for the Federation of American Health Systems (FAHS) in October 1997 which revealed that for-profit hospitals had a favorable (stated as "very favorable" or "somewhat favorable") rating of only 34 percent, compared to much higher marks by not-for-profit hospitals (50 percent), teaching hospitals (57 percent), and community hospitals (62 percent).

Nonetheless, at least one chain, Tenet, has used the opportunity to position itself as the "non-Columbia" alternative. It has taken a highly publicized road of collaboration with its not-for-profit counterparts and has after many years joined the ranks of the American Hospital Association. In the aftermath of the Columbia/HCA debacle, Tenet has effectively lobbied to partner with organizations that were either considering an affiliation with Columbia or considering a partnership with a for-profit institution. "This will likely have a slowdown effect on all the for-profit chains in the short term," Kenneth Abramowitz, health-care industry analyst for Sanford Bernstein, speculated. "The firms will come out of it in two to three years, but in the interim, all the for-profits will suffer because of the bad press surrounding Columbia."

Abramowitz is not alone in his assessment. Tom Scully, president of FAHS, commented that he thought the recent press and the investigations by the government would "temporarily slow down the expansion of the for-profit chains." He went on to compare what is going on in hospitals with what has happened in the banking industry. He added, "It is an inevitable trend [i.e., consolidation]. The investor-owned model will continue. The communities don't want their assets tied up in hospitals, and given the nature of healthcare and the need for capital, the for-profit chains will emerge again and continue their expansion and growth." He noted that within the next two to three years, "When the bad PR wears down, the community hospital executives and boards will look at their options through clearer glasses and many will choose to align with or become partners with for-profit systems."

IMPLICATIONS FOR THE INVESTMENT COMMUNITY

The implosion of Columbia and subsequent slide in its stock price created unease for many investors in hospital stocks. The natural question was whether the investigation would permeate the other chains after the federal agents were done with Columbia. Standing back farther, many wondered whether the for-profit motive could ever be reconciled with the healing mission of hospitals.

Many on the not-for-profit side of the hospital industry shared the concern expressed in this last statement. They argue that profits cannot be a motivator when a patient's health is the product. Yet, to believe that is to believe that when tested the evil nature will always win in any such struggle. For example, if I got a bigger bonus by making cuts that compromised patient care, would I do it? Would you do it? Would most people do it? I believe that the answer is, no. Some people would. Yet, those people would probably do it in a not-for-profit setting as well, and not-for-profit hospitals have bonus systems for administrators, too.

Is there a place for strong management in the hospital industry? Yes! Can this management answer to shareholders without compromising patient care? Yes! When challenged to be more businesslike, the hospital industry has responded in a responsible way. It's interesting to note that when the industry was having double-digit inflation rates in the early 1990s, total hospital profit margins were just over 3 percent and the Consumer Price Index (CPI) was just over 9 percent. By 1996, total hospital profit margins were 7 percent, and the CPI for hospitals had dropped to 4 percent.

As prices dropped, hospitals actually became more efficient. When pushed to the wall, they found ways to cope very well. That's why investors in hospital stocks should be comforted that by investing in strong, ethical management, they're probably benefiting not only their company, but their competitors.

Hospital stocks are not going to be the stars of Wall Street, like a Microsoft or an Intel. However, they will provide steady, noncyclical investments for Joe American, who won't have to blush because he's investing in a "for-profit" hospital company that may take market shares away from a Catholic, Methodist, or Baptist competitor.

IMPLICATIONS FOR COLUMBIA/HCA

Kenneth Abramowitz, one of the healthcare industry's leading analysts, has seen the investor-owned systems rise and fall and rise again. He believes that the impact on Columbia will be a slowdown in its growth, and a change in its style. "It will force them to be less aggressive," Abramowitz predicts. Certainly, Thomas Frist Jr. has already positioned the firm (and the investment community) for such a scenario. He has said time and time again that the firm will concentrate on operations and slow down its rapid growth, as well as its breakneck pace. "If prior management had just slowed down . . .," Frist once mused, in commenting on some of the current problems his besieged firm faces with the government and with the media.

As for the eventual configuration of the firm, there are several scenarios that could play out. One major difference between Frist and Scott is the breadth of their strategic options related to the investment community and the organizational structure of the firm. Scott seemed to know one strategy as related to Wall Street, and that was to grow the business. Increased revenues, volumes, and operating margins were the means by which he and his lieutenants could increase the value of the stock and the worth of the company.

Frist has proven several times that he has a wide portfolio of strategic options related to building the value of his firm, whether it is divesting a portion of the firm (as he did with Healthtrust), taking the firm private (as he did with the LBO), or even making the hospitals not-for-profit (as he considered just before merging with Columbia in 1995).

Frist has proven to be a master at reading the investment option tea leaves and choosing the right strategy that will optimize the value of his considerable holdings, as well as those for the thousands of investors who have entrusted their money with his company. In that sense, he is less of a servant of the whims of the current market, or its financial advisers, and is more likely to march to the long-term drumbeat of the strategy that provides the best outlook for the firm.

He has stated several times that the best way to increase the value of the shareholder is to provide quality patient care. No one can reasonably argue with that statement. However, from a strictly financial standpoint, the option that Frist and his advisers choose for Columbia/HCA will likely be based as much on economic viability as on operational strategy.

Whatever long-term strategy and organizational configuration Frist, Bovender, and the other senior executives at Columbia/HCA choose, the fired-up firm that captured Wall Street's interest and its competitors' envy will never be the same. The overly-driven, take-no-prisoners attitude that characterized Columbia/HCA up until late July of 1997 appears to be as absent from corporate ranks and culture as its champions, Rick Scott and David Vandewater. Eventually, even the name "Columbia" may be a thing of the past.

Ten years (almost to the day) after Scott and Richard Rainwater started the company that would become the juggernaut, Columbia's new chairman and CEO intimated that the name "Columbia" may not be around for the long haul. Ironically, Frist made the prediction in the same city where Columbia was born, Dallas. After speaking to a group of over 200 business leaders at the Fairmont Hotel in late October, (as quoted in *The Dallas Morning News*), Frist said, "The name won't be an important part of our strategy." Columbia's senior vice president of investor relations, Vic Campbell, further elaborated to the *News*, "I doubt that, long term, the *Columbia* name will be the name of the company." With the cessation of the *Columbia* name ends a chapter in one of the most fascinating stories of American business.

Coincidentally, Columbia's brief history has two noteworthy bookends. As noted early in the book, the company was formed on "Black Monday," that economically infamous day (October 19, 1987) when the stock market dropped more than 500 points. Two days following Frist and Campbell's prediction that the Columbia name would eventually be dropped, the nation experienced "Bloody Monday," (October 27, 1997) a day on which the market fell more than it had on Black Monday. However, Bloody Monday was followed by "Correction Tuesday," and the market recovered much of its loss from the prior day.

All of which merely proves two points: First, history tends to repeat itself. Second, Wall Street remains extremely unpredictable and subject to wild swings either way. Both points are relevant to the discussion of for-profit healthcare. In Columbia, the hospital industry was able to observe the renewed and revitalized reincarnation (or at least reconfiguration) of hospital companies once heralded on "the Street." Just as with these predecessor firms, Columbia/HCA is likely to undergo a major metamorphosis that will result in a combination of the scenarios and possibilities described earlier. Through it all, one thing remains certain: The impact of the investor-owned hospital chains is both relevant and refreshing. In an editorial in the October 28, 1997 issue of *The Wall Street Journal,* Dr. Lloyd Krieger, a resident at the University of California, Los Angeles, observed that just as Michael Milken and the junk bonds movement had media criticism, government scrutiny, and public concern, the concept has opened a new wave of investment financing—one that is currently highly used and widely recognized as crucial to America's economic growth. In a similar fashion, the momentum and managerial style that symbolized Columbia/HCA and its aggressive chieftains may prove just as important in transforming the complex and costly healthcare industry. One way or another, Columbia has left its mark on the American landscape.

EPILOGUE

On November 17, 1997, the post-Richard Scott restructuring awaited by Wall Street was unveiled. As many had expected, Dr. Thomas Frist, Jr. and Jack Bovender, Columbia/HCA's CEO and COO respectively, announced their decision to break apart the healthcare behemoth.

"We believe the reorganization is in the best interests of our patients and all of the company's stakeholders, including employees, physicians, local communities, and shareholders." Frist said. In back-to-back conference calls that started with Wall Street analysts, included the media, and extended to Columbia managers and board members of partnerships, Frist and Bovender sketched out the game plan.

The intent of the "internal reorganization," as Frist termed it, was to split the company into five groups. Two of the groups, East and West (led by Jay Grinney and Richard Bracken respectively) consisted of 232 hospitals and would stay with the Nashville corporation. The remaining 108 hospitals would be split into three groups that would eventually be spun off into separate companies or sold. One of those segments, dubbed the America Group (with Jim Fleetwood as its president) would comprise only rural hospitals. The strategy with the America Group was essentially to emulate the highly successful rural hospital chain, Health Management Associates, whose stock traditionally trades at a P/E multiple of 30 or more.

The other two groups, Atlantic and Pacific, each contained just over 40 hospitals and were to be led by David White and Danny Shelton respectively. Interestingly, many of the old HealthTrust hospitals were included in the 108 that were assigned to the "spinoff groups," resulting in a kind of deja-vu for those faclities. However, the 108 also included hospitals in markets where Columbia's goal of building an integrated delivery system was never realized—markets such as Chicago, Boston, and Little Rock.

With the formal announcement of the reorganization, an important chapter closed for Columbia/HCA. The one-time colossus that competed with unparalleled bravado and financial acumen may have fallen short of its goal to change the nation's healthcare system, but it certainly mounted an impressive and highly visible campaign to do so.

ABOUT THE AUTHORS

Sandy Lutz is an author with nearly 15 years' experience covering the business of healthcare. Her first book, *The For-Profit Healthcare Revolution: The Growing Impact of Investor-Owned Health Systems,* chronicled the rise, fall and resurgence of the for-profit hospital industry. It was published in September 1995 by Irwin Professional Books, a division of McGraw-Hill.

Ms. Lutz was Dallas bureau chief of *Modern Healthcare* magazine for nearly 10 years, covering the investor-owned hospital industry as well as a wide range of healthcare finance topics. Following that, she was a healthcare industry analyst for MBD Information Network, Dallas, and a healthcare analyst for Rauscher Pierce Refsnes, an investment bank in Dallas. During the past two years, she has spoken extensively on the topic of investor-owned hospital chains.

Ms. Lutz anchored and wrote a monthly satellite TV news magazine, *Healthcare Business Update,* for HSTN, the nation's largest healthcare satellite network. She also formerly worked for the Memphis Business Journal, the Kansas City Times, and the Lincoln (Neb.) Journal.

She is a journalism graduate of the University of Nebraska-Lincoln, and lives in Arlington, Texas, with her husband and two daughters, Katie, 13, and Sarah, 9.

E. Preston Gee is Senior Vice-President of Marketing and Business Development for Columbia St. David's Healthcare System in Austin, Texas. Prior to joining Columbia St. David's, Mr. Gee worked in senior management for American Medical International (AMI) in Missouri and Sacred Heart General Hospital in Oregon. Before entering the health care field, Mr. Gee spent several years in planning and market development with The Quaker Oats Company.

Mr. Gee is the author of several books on health care strategy, including *The For-Profit Healthcare Revolution,* published in 1995 and *Thriving on Reform,* published in 1994. In addition to his books, Mr. Gee has written numerous articles on industry trends in a variety of professional publications. He is a frequent speaker on health care strategy for professional groups. He is a recipient of *Modern Healthcare Magazine's* "Up and Comers Award" (1994), and received "The Quaker Oats Chairman's Team Award for Excellence" for new product development. Mr. Gee received his MBA and B.S. from Brigham Young University in Provo, Utah.

Mr. Gee and his wife (and six children) live in Austin.

INDEX

Wall Street Journal, The
  critical articles about
    Columbia, 126–127
  "MD vs MBA" article, 129
Wegland, Robert, 121
Wesley Medical Center, HCA
  acquisition of, 20–22
Wessex, 19
Westworld Community Health
  Care, 47

Whiteside, Robert, fraud indict-
  ments, 154–155
Willow Creek Adolescent Center,
  76–77
Wilson, Charles, 155
Wilson, Kemmons, 14
Wong, Herbert, 150

Young, Peter, 128, 188